Unmasking the Sacred Lies

by

Paul A. Cleveland

Boundary Stone • Birmingham, Alabama

ISBN 978-0-9727401-1-1

Library of Congress Control Number : 2008910913

Cover art: Rembrandt Harmenszoon van Rijn: *Belshazzar's Feast*
© The National Gallery, London. Bought with a contribution from the National Art Collections Fund, 1964. Used by permission.

Cover design: Bryan Clendenen

For information about useful reference materials, additional reading lists, and other available resources from Boundary Stone, visit our web site:

http://www.boundarystone.net

Acknowledgements

I have been supported by quite a few people in the process of writing this book and I would like to thank them for their help. First, I would like to thank the American Institute for Economic Research whose generous summer research fellowship provided an excellent environment and the resources to begin the process of putting this book together. Second, I am indebted to Lora Perry whose careful editorial review greatly enhanced the readability of the book. In that regard, I would also like to thank my wife Cathe for doing likewise. Her careful attention to detail significantly improved the manuscript. Needless to say, any remaining errors in the book are my own. Finally, I would like to thank Brian Clendenen for designing the cover and Brandon Robbins for my photograph that appears on the back cover.

The cover art is taken from Rembrandt's famous painting *Belshazzar's Feast* which is based on Daniel's account of the incident that took place during a party held by the last Babylonian king. During that party the king and his guests drank from cups that had once been used in the Israelite temple. As they engaged in their merriment a hand appeared and wrote a message on the wall. The message said that God had weighed the king in a balance and found him wanting. Belshazzar's rule had come to an end. I chose this scene because it points to the final end of all government that is rooted in lies and deception. While there may not appear a hand to write on the wall of the White House at a future state dinner, the truth is that no government can continue on with impunity as it builds more and more on fundamental lies. Indeed, our government likewise will be weighed in the balance and will be found wanting.

With this said, I would like to dedicate this book to my children, Caleb and Katie, whose passion for the truth is inspiring.

Paul A. Cleveland

Contents

Chapter 1: Introduction

Freedom and liberty are familiar words. They are cherished words in America. If you ask any American if he is committed to upholding freedom and liberty he will no doubt say yes. But what do these words mean? Judging from the changing nature of public policy in America it should be clear that the meaning attached to these words today is far different from what the nation's founders thought. Today, freedom and liberty tend to be understood to be a license to do whatsoever one wants to do, while avoiding any negative consequences that might be associated with such action. This is certainly not the understanding of freedom and liberty that was held by the early Americans. They knew that people are responsible for their actions and should be made accountable. They understood that certain actions resulted in certain consequences and argued on that basis that people are responsible to bear the consequences of their own behavior either for their good or for their ill. Therefore, they conceived of freedom and liberty not as a license, but as the context in which human action is carried out. They believed that the process of human action in which people are made accountable for the consequences of their behavior would tend to lead people to do those things that they ought to do because of the negative outcomes associated with the alternative.

Today's popular notion of freedom and liberty, that a person should be free to behave in any way he likes without suffering the consequences of his behavior, has spawned a massive welfare and warfare federal government that ultimately destroys human freedom and responsibility. The new conception reduces the value of any individual human being to nothing. In a very real sense, each person is reduced to a position of forced servitude in which he labors for the benefit of the state and those who are politically well connected. Thus, the average person is made a slave of the political elites. He is willing to accept this situation because he is no longer responsible for many of his actions in the strict sense. Instead, he is made a perpetual ward of the state. In short, his real liberty is truncated. Moreover, most Americans today accept this new position because the circumstances of life are relatively comfortable. Regrettably, the general acceptance of the modern view of liberty cuts away at the very foundations of civilization that enable them to live in such comfort. Eventually, the circumstances of life will deteriorate as political tyranny and despotism increases thus robbing society of its general well-being. That is the long run result of extending the freedom to some to do whatsoever they desire at the moment by imposing the costs of their action on others. Eventually, as more people begin to exercise this freedom and the costs of their actions multiply, such political manipulation will be revealed as a fraud.

In the course of human history, civilizations have come and gone. In the ebb and flow of time, nations and empires were built up only to fall later into destruction and ruin. Observers of history have always pondered the reasons for greatness and have looked for the reasons of decay and destruction. In modern times the United States of America has risen to prominence. One particular manifestation of this greatness is the material affluence that the citizens of the U.S. enjoy. It has been and is far greater than that attained by any people beforehand. However, there is good evidence that the foundations that undergird our success are steadily eroding away. This is happening as people in our society exchange lies for the truths that were once readily affirmed. These lies promote certain kinds of policies and behaviors that will eventually lead to the demise of our material prosperity. Typically, grand civilizations do not die overnight. Rather, they wither away bit by bit until those things that once made them great are no longer present in any form or fashion. The purpose of this book is to provide an economic history of the public policies pursued in the United States and to point out how these policies compromise or confirm foundational principles. The aim of the book is to shed light on the underlying lies which threaten the foundations upon which the nation's achievements are based.

Toward this end, an examination of some of the fundamental economic principles that were once hallmarks of the American order needs to be made. Among the principles which were most responsible for the material success of this nation was the national commitment to private property and free trade.[1] I state the commitment to private property and free trade as a single principle because one cannot exist without the other. It simply cannot be said that people are free to trade if they do not have title to their property. Likewise, we cannot say that people possess clear title to their property unless they are able to do whatever they want to do with it.

While much is still made of the American commitment to the principle of free trade and private property, it is increasingly done only in a rhetorical sense because much of the substance of this standard has been compromised. The popular understanding of what the commitment is has changed dramatically in the past hundred years or so and is today only a faint reflection of what it once was. So much is this the case that one wonders whether or not it is truthful to say that Americans are predominantly committed to private property and free trade. To get a better understanding of why this is the case, it is necessary to examine what such a commitment entails. From a good understanding of the principle of private property, we can then begin to examine how the popular views of today have evolved. This will be done by examining the development of the various public policies that have been adopted. In this process, we will unmask the sacred lies that have been popularly spread.

Property Rights

One of the obvious facts about the human condition is

---

[1] For an excellent empirical examination that demonstrates the connection between free trade and economic prosperity see James Gwartney and Robert Lawson's, *Economic Freedom of the World Annual Report*, available at www.fraserinstitute.org.

that we are creatures who possess minds so that we can think, will, and act. In addition, we are physical creatures who need material sustenance for survival. As such, the first human beings encountered a world in which they had to work to produce the goods that sustained them and provided for their satisfactions such as they were. Given these basic facts about human existence, it would seem that nothing is clearer than the existence of property and of the inherent human right to one's personal property. If I exert myself to plant and tend a blackberry bush it would seem obvious that the bush and the berries to be harvested from it would be mine. Beyond this, it would also seem clear that since human beings are capable of thought, and since we are naturally free to think and to act as we see fit, that such freedom to live and the liberty to act are also fundamental rights of the person. For this reason, it can be concluded that people possess the right to life and the right to liberty as well as the right to property. Furthermore, rationality requires that these rights must be understood to extend to all persons so that one should not violate the human rights of another person. And, since property is essential for survival, a person should not violate the property rights of another person either. This is the essence of the rational case for the existence of property rights. It was articulated by John Locke in his *Two Treatises on Government*, and it was affirmed by the American founders.[2]

While the case for property rights is compelling, it has not been universally understood or accepted. In fact, the history of the human race is littered with examples where these basic human rights have been denied. Such denial of the rights of others results primarily from the strong incentive that men have, and have so often acted upon, to obtain the things that they desire at someone else's expense. In the blackberry bush example, there have always been people who desire to eat the blackberries off another man's bush without giving him anything in return. Indeed, it is well said that theft was the first labor saving device.

---

[2] John Locke, *Two Treatises on Government.*

For whatever reason one may conclude, the facts of the matter reveal that men are not generally prone to respect the rights of others.

All people are born into this world with a host of needs that must be met if they are to survive. In addition, there are obstacles that must be overcome if those needs are to be satisfied.[3] As a result, people must work to overcome the obstacles of life to satisfy their needs and wants. This fact means that there are only a few ways that people can obtain the goods they desire.

1. They can rely solely upon their own productive efforts.
2. They can produce something desired by others and trade it for the things they want.
3. They can receive what they desire as a gift from someone else.
4. They can steal what they want from others.[4]

This last activity uses force or fraud in a way that denies the freedom and liberty of the people from whom the goods are stolen and, therefore, violates natural human rights. Using force against another person to take his possessions robs him of his liberty. Likewise, deceiving another person to gain his possessions when he would not have relinquished them is to rob him of his liberty. Nevertheless, if we can learn anything from history it is that man has always had a marked propensity for this kind of human action.

It is important to note, however, that it would be impossible for everyone to steal from everyone else as a means of survival. If everyone attempted to live at the expense of everyone else, and no one engaged in any productive activity, then there would be nothing to steal for nothing would have been

---

[3] For an excellent essay on obstacles see, Frederic Bastiat, "Obstacle and Cause," *Economic Sophisms*, available at www.econlib.org.

[4] For an expanded treatment of the ways that people can get what they want see, Clarence Carson, *Basic Economics*, (Phenix City: American Textbook Committee, 1988), Chapter 7.

produced. If stealing is to provide for one's needs, there must first be something to steal and that means that someone must have worked to produce something. For this reason, the large majority of people have always relied on their own labor for survival. Only a minority of people have been able to live by thievery. Just the same, the thieves of this world have always posed a continual problem. Namely, thieves hinder the material success that might be enjoyed because their actions are a direct attack on property and it would be better if they gave up on thievery and engaged in some productive enterprise instead. For this reason, people have always sought to protect themselves from thieves.

Among the earliest examples of such protection was the development of farming communities in the river valleys where human civilizations first flourished. These communities provided the opportunity for their members to enjoy the material gains to be had from specialization and trade. They also provided a means by which the members of the community could protect themselves from roaming gangs of bandits. Moreover, these communities provided a means of adjudicating disputes among the local residents. Within these communities the use of force to provide defensive protection of property and to secure the local peace was collectively organized. As a result, these communities spawned the first forms of government.

While the need for government is to provide for the protection of human rights, the essence of government is that it is an institution that uses force to accomplish its ends. To enforce compliance with its orders, government must be able to impose penalties, and this necessarily implies the use of force. In fact, that is all that the institution of government can ever be. Given this fact, and given that the need for it rises because men do not naturally respect the human rights of others, the reality of government in practice is that its use of power has typically not been confined to its appropriate end. Instead, throughout history, it might be noted that stealing has been most effectively accomplished by those using government power. For instance, the early empires provide excellent examples of people who rose to prominence in government and then used their positions of power to expand their political control over others. This allowed these leaders to live lives of privilege at the expense of other human beings. The Assyrian Empire illustrates this very well. The Assyrians were people of Semitic origin who began as farmers in the upper Mesopotamia river valley. They initially developed a skilled military for the purpose of protecting the community. However, in the course of time, the Assyrians realized that they could use their military prowess to effectively raid neighboring communities. By marching their army around to different communities and giving the people in each place the option to either pay tribute or to suffer annihilation, the Assyrians were able to expand their political control over more and more people. In short, they lived at the expense of the labor of others by subjugating conquered people to themselves.

The same sort of activity is of course true of the modern period as well. However, the modern period is also characterized by a marked denial of the natural right to property. In fact, many accept as legitimate the notion that property rights only exist because governments have created laws that established them. Within this philosophical framework, it has been argued that these laws are responsible for the exploitation of human labor throughout history. Such was the essence of the case against the free market made by Karl Marx in the nineteenth century. As a result of this kind of argumentation, the modern period has been marked by a good deal of socialistic experimentation aimed at undermining established property rights and over throwing the rule of property right law. This policy was most actively pursued in countries where communist revolutions took place. In addition, this viewpoint is behind the many policies of democratic socialists in the rest of the world.

However, the reality is, as has already been shown, that property exists as an outgrowth of human nature itself and cannot be destroyed. This is what the communists in the former Soviet Union came to realize. Namely, they could not destroy property. They could only redistribute it from one group to another via a complex government structure that actually exploited human labor. In effect, those with political power were attempting to live as thieves off the forced servitude of the people at large in the Soviet Union. However, like all parasites, if the host upon whom they feed is killed, then they die as well. In the course of time, this is exactly what took place causing the Soviet system to collapse.

The collapse of communism would seem to provide all the evidence needed to reaffirm the importance of property rights and the rule of law in society. In addition, it should be clear that societies that secure property rights provide the context within which the greatest material prosperity is made possible. Indeed, much has been made of the need for people around the world to adopt free market economies in their own countries in order to expand world trade. However, it is also true that many western countries are continuing to pursue their own socialistic experimentations. That is, the tenets of socialism have not been completely abandoned. Rather, socialism can be found in various forms throughout the world. The United States has not been immune to the spread of socialistic ideas. In fact, the spread of the central notion behind all socialism is the fundamental lie that threatens the economic vitality of America. As one would expect, wherever it is found embedded in governmental policies, it is creating economic problems and hindering material prosperity because it is in essence a governmental means of systematically violating property rights.

Trade

To understand why private property is fundamental to economic success, one must understand the essential benefit of trade. One key factor that is helpful in understanding the events that shaped men's lives is the ebb and flow of the continuing development of commercial relationships among the various peoples of the world. In short, the expansion of trade among people is of great importance in gaining a clear understanding of human civilization. For this reason, it is important to understand why it is that people trade in the first place and then to understand the context in which trade flourishes. Finally, it is important to understand why it is that men so often short-circuit the prospects of trade by way of political control.

The reason why people trade among one another is really quite simple. In fact, it is one of the first principles of economics. Namely, people engage in trade because there are mutual benefits that arise from it. This is a world of immense diversity. From one place to another there are vast differences in climates and in resources available. One region might be well suited to growing apple trees, while another is better suited for citrus production, and still another best suited for growing grains of various sorts. In addition, some minerals may be found in certain regions, while others are only available elsewhere.

Beyond the diversity of terrains, of climates, and of materials that are at hand for productive enterprise, there are also immense differences among people. Some people are naturally athletic, while others possess more acute intellectual skills. Furthermore, some people are born with the gift of dexterity that enables them to perform intricate tasks with great ease, while others among us possess abilities that are best suited for use in other endeavors. And beyond all of the differences associated with the natural world, and beyond the differences in talents that human beings possess, there is also a diversity of ends that people pursue. While one person might find fulfillment in collecting classic sports cars, someone else might think that is insignificant relative to his desire for building a new house.

Emerging out of the vast numbers of differences among resources and individuals, there exist vast numbers of opportunities for people to gain mutual benefits by way of trading goods with one another. In essence, the differences in the ends that people pursue, coupled with their differences in talents and the differences in resources that can be used to achieve their ends, give rise to differences in how people subjectively evaluate the usefulness of various economic goods. As a result, it is possible that when two people come together, each person will desire what the other person has more than the good he already possesses. If apple trees grow well on one person's property, no matter how much he enjoys them, there is a limit to how many he can consume. Eventually his neighbor's abundant vegetables look increasingly appealing. In this case, both parties can be made better off by exchanging their goods. This is essentially what is taking place in every economic transaction.

The only feature that complicates the matter is the invention of money. As trade continued to progress in the early years of human history, money emerged as a means of facilitating trade in an indirect way. But, money does not eliminate the fact that people trade goods for goods. Money merely allows people to accomplish such trades in an indirect manner. The importance of indirect trade can be understood when we think about the difficulty involved in bringing two people together who each want what the other one has. In such circumstances, the extent of trade would be quite limited because there would always have to be a double coincidence of wants. But if people could agree on a common medium of exchange, perhaps some good that is readily accepted by everyone, then trade can expand in much more complex ways. This, in fact, is what happened as people more and more adopted gold and silver as commodity monies for the purpose of engaging in indirect trade. Yet, in the final analysis, the essence of trade remains an exchange of goods for goods even though it is accomplished in this roundabout way.

Trade has expanded as the natural barriers to it have been overcome. These barriers include the costs of gaining information about what might be traded, the costs of transporting goods from one place to another, and the costs of communicating between potential trading partners. It must be noted that information is limited. As a result, some exchanges do not occur simply because the potential trading partners do not recognize the opportunities at hand. That is, commerce can only expand when people in one place are familiar with people in another such that both realize the benefits to be gained from trade. This means that both parties would have to recognize the opportunity. In the history of things, such information has been accumulated in such a way that the tendency has been for the amount of trade to increase over time. As information improved, commercial relationships expanded.

Beyond the possession of better information, so too have transportation and communication systems improved. In fact, these better modes of transportation and communication have generally given rise to better information. Discoveries have been made and inventions have been developed that served to reduce these fundamental obstacles to trade. As better means of overcoming the barriers to commerce were discovered, trade increased. An example of this fact can be found in Vasco da Gama's discovery of an all water route from Europe to East Asia around the tip of Africa. Prior to this discovery, trade between Europeans and Asians could only be completed by way of hauling goods over some combination of water and land. While merchants sought the most direct and efficient routes, these were difficult and added to the costs of trade. When the new water route was opened, goods were more readily transported between these parts of the world. As a result of the reduction in the cost of transporting goods, the trade between these regions of the world increased rapidly. This is but one of countless instances in human history where discoveries or inventions of some sort provided an impetus for an expansion of commercial relationships between the various peoples of this world.

To put the matter simply, the expansion of trade is fundamentally associated with human progress. However, merchants have always been subjected to numerous hardships that they must overcome to accomplish their commercial enterprise. The distances over which goods had to be transported were often long, and the weather and other natural elements were often harsh and unpredictable. In addition, there have always been people who have sought to gain their livelihood in this world by merely taking what they wanted from someone else.

Therefore, the merchant had to overcome not only the natural
barriers to trade, but those created artificially by other people as
well. Pirates, bandits, and other gangs of thieves have preyed
upon unsuspecting merchants throughout human history. As a
result, merchants and their customers in the trading centers
around the world had to be ready to defend themselves and their
property from being attacked and plundered.

As mentioned earlier, it was for this reason that
communities developed governments and formed armies to
defend themselves and their property. In this way, the power of
defense was centralized. Unfortunately, power can be used for
either defensive purposes or for offensive purposes and
governments have historically shown their propensity to use force
in illegitimate ways. That is, in the course of human events,
governments have often been guilty of using the power at hand
to plunder one group of people for the benefit of some other
group. In fact, throughout history, government officials have
abused the power given to them and have used it as a means for
doing the very thing that they were supposed to prevent. Namely,
countless cases can be cited where rulers have used their
positions of authority to plunder the property of their subjects
and of other peoples as well. Therefore, one of the perennial
problems of expanding free trade is the need to limit the use of
government power to its appropriate realm of defending life,
liberty, and property. While there have been numerous political
experiments that aimed at securing justice by limiting
government power, there has never been a case where the use of
power was kept to its appropriate realm. Instead, the various
political experiments have met with greater or lesser success.

Just the same, the natural barriers to trade continue to be
overcome in the modern era. In fact, modern transportation and
communication systems allow for people around the world to
greatly expand their commercial relationships and so the benefits
of exchange have tended to proliferate. Nonetheless, this
proliferation of benefits has been hindered by government action
that is used to extend special privileges to some by imposing costs

on others. In fact, all of the socialistic experiments of the modern era provide excellent examples of this problem.

Human Action

In laying the groundwork for our investigation of the evolution of public policy in America, the importance of private property and trade has already been clearly articulated. What remains is a more complete discussion of the nature of human action and the development of the framework within which our policy analysis will proceed. As already mentioned, human beings are volitional creatures who think, plan and act. When a person acts, he acts with purpose to achieve some desirable end that he has in mind. Following the work of Carl Menger, Ludwig von Mises, and Murray Rothbard, it is asserted that people always act in such purposeful ways and this invariably implies certain things. For instance, only individual people act. There is no such thing as the collective. Such groups are only individual people choosing to act together. In addition, people will only act in ways in which they believe that their action will achieve some desired result. Moreover, the acting person always must choose between competing options in his action because his resources at hand are scarce. In this regard, human choices are always understood to be made at the margin in a real world where the individual faces real restraints that limit his actions. For example, time is always a limiting factor because it is scarce for every human being.

The extension of these ideas of human action in the economic science has proceeded in many directions. The analysis presented here will employ an understanding of both the Austrian knowledge problem as well as the notion of special interest politics as developed in the public choice tradition. The Austrian knowledge problem recognizes that politicians and bureaucrats simply do not have the information needed to effectively carry out their jobs even if they were making a good faith effort to do so.[5] This is true because the information they need arises only in the context of an ongoing market. The market process provides that information via resource prices. These prices give immediate feedback to decision makers about the wisdom of their decisions. Profits indicate wise choices in resource allocations while losses point to the need to reassess one's activities. However, since government officials operate outside of the market, no such process exists that would allow them to evaluate their activities. As a result they tend to become complacent even as they assume that they are experts about things they may know little or nothing about. In short, central planners may be ignorant of their own ignorance. While private planners may also be ignorant, they have the incentive to overcome it and can use market prices as a mechanism to effectively do so. Conversely, central planners have no such incentive. They can claim to have special knowledge even in their ignorance and use that claim to extend their power and control. In fact, their own failures can be easily pointed to as a reason for increasing and extending their power and control in order to insure some supposed future success in central planning.[6] That is, their own failure may serve to deepen their faith in their own illusory understanding of what they think they know. In this case, ignorance and failure can breed even greater ignorance and failure. Even if government planners understood their ignorance, they would likely continue to make plans and decisions as if they knew what they were doing. They would defend their actions by saying that they were just doing their jobs.

The second approach that will be used to analyze policies is public choice theory. Public choice theorists have done a good job in recent years of pointing out that the political process is one that will inevitably be dominated by special interests if those involved act in self-seeking ways. This follows from the fact that

---

[5] Israel M. Kirzner, *The Meaning of the Market Process: Essays in the Development of Modern Austrian Economics,* (London: Routledge, 1992).

[6] Paul A. Cleveland and Jared R. Price, "The Failure of Federal Aviation Administration Regulation," *The Independent Review,* Summer 2003, pp. 53-63.

any single voter has little say in the outcome of an election and, hence, each voter has little incentive to overcome his ignorance of political activities. The costs associated with gaining sufficient information to cast an informed vote is prohibitively high given the benefits of such efforts are not likely to affect the outcome. In turn, those who are most politically connected can manipulate the system for their personal ends. In this context, it pays politicians to cater to certain special interest groups and obscure the facts surrounding the kinds of policies they support. As Charlotte Twight has argued, the "universal tactic" of politicians in providing special favors to friends is to do so by raising the transaction costs associated with informed voting.[7] That is, politicians invariably employ an array of political strategies that make it more difficult and costly for the average voter to peer behind the legislative process to evaluate properly the governmental proposals. In turn, while the average voter would be opposed to most of the legislation properly understood, his inability to access the information needed and to organize against the political action allows the process to run amuck. The costs associated with trying to understand exactly why certain policies will only benefit the favored few at the expense of the public good are too high to warrant the individual voter's attention given that his single vote is not likely to affect the outcome. The result of this process becomes a quagmire of laws and programs that grows in many twisted and perverted ways. In addition, the size and scope of government grows unabated. The problem with this kind of growth is that it has led to the destruction of past civilizations. For example, Rome fell because it had taxed itself into oblivion and no one cared any longer to save her.[8]

In this book, I assume that both the Austrian knowledge problem and the special interest problem impact the current

---

[7] Charlotte A. Twight, *Dependent on D. C.: The Rise of Federal Control Over the Lives of Ordinary Americans*, (New York: Palgrave, 2002).

[8] For further reading on the subject see Charles Adams, *Those Dirty Rotten Taxes: The Tax Revolts that Built America*, (New York: The Free Press, 1998) or Paul A. Cleveland, *Understanding the Modern Culture Wars: The Essentials of Western Civilization*, (Birmingham, AL: Boundary Stone, 2003).

political environment. That is, some officials may think of themselves as serving the public good as best they can, but since they are so ill informed about the issues, they are easily duped by the special interests groups who often have cohorts inside government itself. In addition, those who are well meaning in the system are often unaware of how their own ideas of government have been molded by the political process itself. The result has been an expansion in the power and scope of government beyond the imagination of the nation's founders. In my approach to study of policy, I recognize the value of Robert Higgs analysis.[9] Higgs noted that the historical process has

> ...three critical aspects: first, it involved not just greater spending, taxing, and employing by the government, but more fundamentally, an extension in the scope of the government's effective authority over economic decision making; second, this expansion of authority occurred largely during a few episodes of societal crisis, especially during the world wars and the Great Depression; and third, the growth of the scope of governmental activities paralleled a widely noticed change in prevailing ideology.

The important point that Higgs is making is that government authorities have used opportune occasions to consolidate power and control. These officials had to persuade a significant proportion of the population that they needed new powers to deal with each crisis. Acquiescence to this appeal has resulted in the rapid expansion in the size and scope of the government far beyond the natural law limitations imposed by the U.S. Constitution. With this in mind, an examination of the ongoing development of public policy in America can begin.

---

[9] Robert Higgs, "Crisis, Bigger Government, and Ideological Change: Two Hypotheses on the Ratchet Phenomenon," 1985, available at www.independent.org.

Chapter 2: Fiscal Policy

Fiscal policy is used to refer to the general direction of the government's spending and taxing of its citizens. This direction is affected by the popular perception of the purpose and role of government in society. In the history of the United States there has been an ongoing shift in the popular conception of government and this has likewise resulted in a shift in the nation's fiscal policy. More and more, the American people have replaced their initial understanding that government had a narrow and limited role in society with the idea that government is responsible for the material well-being of its citizens. This change occurred as socialistic and collectivistic ideas of utopian society proliferated and increased in the latter part of the nineteenth century and continued to gain sway in the twentieth century. This coupled with a changing political landscape that aimed at obfuscating the issues of economic reality have served to reinforce this change in perspective. As a result of the spread of collectivist and statist views, the levels of spending and taxing have increased dramatically.

Stephen Moore has shown what has happened to federal outlays in real terms over the course of the nation's history.[10] Real federal outlays in 1990 dollars rose from $0.1 billion in 1800 to $8.3 billion in 1900. When that number is adjusted for the increase in population size he found that per capita government expenditures in this hundred year period increased from $16 to $109 in real terms. However, during the twentieth century expenditures climbed dramatically. By 1992 real expenditures had risen to $1,450 billion in 1992 which represented per capita expenditures of $4,760.[11] The federal budget for 2003 expended in excess of 2 trillion dollars and was

---

[10] Stephen Moore, "The Growth of Government in America," *Ideas on Liberty*, April 1993, pp. 124-136.
[11] Ibid, 124-126.

expected to climb each year into the future.[12] These increases in expenditures represent an exorbitant increase in the size and scope of government. To pay the bill, taxes have likewise been steadily and significantly increased throughout the past hundred years or so. In addition, new forms of taxes have been created to hide the costs of government largess.

In the early years of American history, the motivating and prevailing understanding was that there was a necessary but limited role for government to play in society. The founders thought government action was primarily to be aimed at providing protection for private property, providing for the national defense, and mitigating disputes that could not be settled any other way. In fact, the founders maintained an overarching fear of government and sought specifically to limit it by limiting its scope of action. As Thomas Jefferson put the matter in his first inaugural address,

> A wise and frugal government...shall restrain men from injuring one another, shall leave them otherwise free to regulate their own pursuits of industry and improvement, and shall not take from the mouth of labor the bread it has earned. This is the sum of good government.

In an effort to effectively secure a limited role for government, the founders crafted the Constitution to spell out the specific kinds of action that it could undertake. As James Madison stated in a speech he gave at the Virginia Ratifying Convention,

> [T]he powers of the federal government are enumerated; it can only operate in certain cases; it has legislative powers on defined and limited objects, beyond which it cannot extend its jurisdiction.

It was in this context that the United States as a nation

---

[12] Clyde Wayne Crews, "Ten Thousand Commandments: An Annual Snapshot of the Federal Regulatory State," 2003, available at www.cato.org.

began. Despite the clearly stated principles of good government, there were examples of egregious errors. For example the existence of slavery, the periodic institutions of protectionist tariffs, and the occasional subsidies provided for certain businesses all violated the stated principles of just government. Moreover, there were those people, such as Alexander Hamilton, who pushed for greater central control. Nevertheless, these violations and vested interests were more or less held in check and limited by the Constitution. To be sure, there were always politicians and other governmental officials wishing to obfuscate the Constitution for their own benefit and certainly some succeeded in doing so. Yet, the damage that they inflicted tended to be limited and temporary.

One of the first lasting departures from limited government occurred with the election of Abraham Lincoln. As Tom DiLorenzo noted, Lincoln successfully sidestepped the Constitution in order to expand governmental authority.[13] As DiLorenzo put the matter,

> Lincoln will always be remembered as the Great Emancipator. But he was also the Great Centralizer, whose policies did much to undermine the decentralized, federal system established by the Founders.[14]

During his administration there was a serious national crisis in which Constitutional protections were abated and political power was extended. Following Higgs' argument of how such crises lead to shifts in ideological understandings, this set in motion a path of political change aimed at replacing some economic freedom with central planning. To be sure, others had tried this earlier.[15] Certainly, Alexander Hamilton was in favor of

---

[13] Thomas J. DiLorenzo, "The Great Centralizer: Abraham Lincoln and the War Between the States," *The Independent Review*, Fall 1998, pp. 243-271.

[14] Ibid, 244.

[15] Robert Higgs, "Crisis, Bigger Government, and Ideological Change: Two Hypotheses on the Ratchet Phenomenon," 1985, available at www.independent.org.

a strong central government that would in some sense plan the economy as was evident by his desire to establish and maintain a national bank. However, his efforts were largely ineffective and a free market mentality remained generally pervasive in the nation. Lincoln's political views were shaped by his admiration of Henry Clay who labored in the Whig party for years. Clay shared Hamilton's view and his ideas were embraced by Lincoln. He favored a strong central government, protective tariffs, and centralized banking. The difference between Lincoln and his predecessors was that his efforts had a more lasting effect on the nation, while the successes of those before him were temporary. He, thus, set in motion the political activity that would eventually bring about the shared vision of promoting mercantilism in the U.S.

Prior to Lincoln's election, there were two main issues that worked against the maintenance of limited government in America because the accepted views of the people and the policies adopted generally violated the principles of justice that undergirded the American system. These issues were slavery and tariffs. Among advocates of limited government and free trade this was well understood. As Frederic Bastiat wrote in 1849 in his famous essay, *The Law*:

> ...in the United States, there are two issues—and only two—that have always endangered the public peace. What are these two issues? They are slavery and tariffs... Slavery is a violation, by law, of liberty. The protective tariff is a violation, by law, of property.[16]

As already mentioned, Hamilton and his followers had always wanted to shape American government and public policy after the mercantilistic practices that had long been the hallmark of European life. However, the Hamiltonians faced strong opposition from others who maintained a free market understanding of how the economy functioned and saw such a

---

[16] Frederic Bastiat, *The Law*, available at www.econlib.org.

stance as inherently linked to the political freedom they had fought for. While the Hamiltonians achieved some successes, they tended to be short lived until Lincoln's presidency and the Civil War.

When Lincoln was elected president, it was clear that he strongly favored a large increase in tariffs that was being pushed for during the election year. This tariff would essentially protect industrial business interests in the Northern states at the expense of business interests in the Southern states. Under this plan Southerners would be forced to pay higher prices for the goods they needed while Northern businessmen would enjoy governmental protection from foreign competition. In other words, Southerners would be made to bear the brunt of taxation to pay for a larger central government and to provide special privileges for Northern business interests. Southern democrats had fought against such taxation for years and had largely succeeded up to this point in time. However, with Lincoln's election, it was clear to Southern leaders that their efforts would no longer prevail even though they believed that such taxation was unconstitutional because it was not proportioned among the states as the Constitution clearly stated that taxes must be. As a result, they believed that they had the right to secede from the union on these grounds. Of course their efforts to set up their own free trade zone failed and the result was the first significant breach of limited government. That is not to suggest that slavery was not also a breach of the ideals of limited government or that it was an unimportant factor leading to war, since surely it was. But slavery was not the only issue at stake. As it was, while the North embraced the correct position on the issue of slavery, it adopted the wrong view on the economy. Likewise, while the South had the correct view on the economy, it held the wrong view on the slave issue. Therefore, since the North won, the Civil War resolved the issue of slavery setting in motion a change in the political climate. While the elimination of slavery was good, this change has tended to erode economic freedom in America and has resulted in an ongoing expansion of government taxing and spending.

Both during and after the Lincoln administration, the federal government significantly expanded its involvement in private affairs. As they had wanted to do for some time, the Whigs (who were by this time known as the Republicans) justified all sorts of special favor, pork-barrel projects on the basis of a distorted reading of the general welfare clause of the Constitution. It is clear from James Madison's correspondence that the phrase was never meant to be a blank check on which government could extend favors based on the assertion that such action would "promote the general welfare." But, that is the way that the Republicans wanted to interpret the phrase and since they held the bulk of the political power after the war they were able to expand government favors to certain private interests. As such, business subsidies and other corporate welfare policies were adopted that transferred wealth from taxpayers to those who were politically well connected. These transfers attracted all sorts of private interests who used their scarce resources to lobby the government for various political privileges and favors.

Economists refer to this kind of activity as rent seeking since these efforts are wholly wasteful. Rent seeking is essentially an effort to gain an advantage by lobbying Congress for political privilege. It aims to establish laws that limit people's choices. Rather than concentrating on how best to serve his clientele, the rent seeker attempts to hold his customers hostage by restricting their options. To promote their privilege rent seekers often resort to high sounding rhetoric that is intended to mask the real agenda. In actuality, the rent seeker aims to make his customers serve his needs and desires on his terms. As such, these activities merely seek to make customers the slaves of the politically successful privilege seeker.

Nonetheless, corporate rent seekers began to descend upon Washington in pursuit of the new governmental privileges that were being offered. To pay for the new pork, as well as for the war itself, an income tax was imposed upon the people as being necessary in that time of national emergency. While the tax was eventually ended, it served as a first step in gaining acceptance of the idea. Within a few years another income tax was imposed which was eventually struck down when the Supreme Court ruled that it was unconstitutional.

Beyond the politics of that day, the latter part of the nineteenth century was also a time in which the writings of the romanticists prospered and in which the ideas of utopians and various other social reformers spread. The combination of the political circumstances following the Civil War, along with the prevalence of these ideas, provided an opportunity for the greater centralization of government power and the Progressive movement was born. Social reformers of one stripe or another began to agitate for government to be more involved in fixing one kind or another of the various social ills of that day. Many of these proposals fell upon deaf ears among a people who remained more or less committed to the ideals of personal liberty and autonomous human action. Nevertheless, they did receive more of a hearing than they would have apart from the policies that had been undertaken beginning with Lincoln.

In addition to the changes brought about by the Civil War, there were other changes taking place as well that allowed the reformers to play upon the people's fears. For example, entrepreneurial activity and capital accumulation allowed some individuals to amass sizable fortunes by operating large scale enterprises. While some companies were gaining size as a result of state privilege, others were successful primarily because they utilized large scale capital to cut the costs of production.[17] As a result, they were able to offer customers equal or better products at lower prices than had been available previously. This was a boon for consumers who discovered a wider variety of cheaper products to choose from. However, such activities did undercut the business opportunities of those who could not compete on the same scale. This situation provided an opportunity for the

---

[17] Burton W. Folsom, *The Myth of the Robber Barons*, (Herndon, VA: Young America's Foundation, 1991).

centralizers to play upon the fears of ordinary citizens in order to extend governmental power and control.

Fear is a powerful motivator. When people are afraid, they may respond in ways that are neither rational nor moral in search of some kind of security. When people abandon their sense of morality and their good reason in order to gain security, they do not do so on a wholesale basis. Rather, they abandon their principles at the margin. Indeed, that was what was beginning to happen. The centralizers could, therefore, play upon the fears of the people to extend government powers in ways that would have been thought awful only a few years beforehand. This process succeeds in eroding both morality and rationality because the consequences are rarely as immediate and as hard as people might have thought to be the case. For instance, when a person acts against a moral principle for the first time, he realizes afterwards that lightning did not come down from the sky and that the immediate consequences were not as bad as he might have imagined them to be. In fact, he might even believe after the fact that his compromise served his greater good. The drug addict living in the slums and spending most of his waking hours either searching for or doing drugs did not come to that place after his first illicit use of them. In fact, his first use was most likely exceedingly pleasurable which is why he used the drugs again. The addiction and the destruction of a drug addict's life is something that happens slowly over time.

This is the way it is when people search for economic security through central planning. Initially, one's efforts to gain that security by political action may even appear to work for those in search of it. When such security is achieved, the beneficiary rarely acknowledges that his gain was gotten at someone else's expense. Thus, from his point of view, the effort seems to be a success and this sets in motion future efforts to extend the kind of safety and security first gained. Needless to say, that any expansion in government power and control will require additional finances and that is what happened. After the Civil War, the federal government began efforts to find new sources of funding. This search for revenue went on unabated and marked a significant change in the direction of fiscal policy in the nation.

The expansion in power rarely followed a smooth path. Rather, circumstances along life's way provided opportunities for clear leaps in the magnitude of government power and control. Eventually, the successes of the proponents of Progressive policies resulted in the next great water shed for the consolidation of power which took place during Wilson's administration in beginning of the twentieth century. Woodrow Wilson's pursuit of consolidating power got a boost from the outset of his term with the passage of the Sixteenth Amendment to the Constitution in February of 1913. The amendment legalized the federal income tax in America. In addition to this new legal source of revenue, his efforts at extending state control were also enhanced when he signed the Federal Reserve Act later that year. The act created the Federal Reserve System which effectively cartelized banking in the U.S. This second fact will be of more interest in the next chapter which focuses on monetary policy. What can be said now is that throughout history rulers of all types have understood the benefit of controlling the money.

In 1914, World War I broke out in Europe and Wilson, despite his words to the contrary, began looking for a way to enter it.[18] In 1917, the U.S. entered the war and the Wilson administration maneuvered politically to establish a state-corporate collectivism to manage the nation's resources for the effort. As Higgs pointed out, the effort was more a move to reshape the nation's conception of the role of government than it was a need for waging the war.[19] After all, the government could have simply contracted with the necessary private enterprises and parties for the needed resources and could have paid for the effort through its abilities to collect taxes. Nevertheless, Wilson's strategy was to conceal the cost of the

---

[18] Ralph Raico, "FDR: The Man, the Leader, the Legacy," April 2001, available at www.independent.org.
[19] Op. cit

whole affair and impose taxes by restricting the individual's liberty. This has been a political strategy that has been with us on a large scale ever since. The administration justified its actions as needed in order to wage a more focused war on America's enemies.

> Besides wholesale violations of economic freedom, the war years saw the brutal suppression of freedom of speech and of the press, especially by means of the Espionage and Sedition Acts. Anyone who voiced dissent from the government's line was branded a traitor and treated accordingly.[20]

As for the initial income tax, it provided the opportunity for political actors to achieve their objectives by playing social classes against one another. As a matter of fact, it was class warfare that made the passage of the amendment possible to begin with. It had been promoted as a tax that would only be levied against the very rich to generate the much needed funding for programs that had become generally popular. Judging from the initial tax schedule this seemed clear to everyone. Adjusted for inflation and stated in 1994 dollars, the tax schedule levied no tax on the first $44,776 of income that a single individual filer earned or the first $59,701 that a married couple earned. After that a progressive tax was applied beginning with a marginal rate of 1 percent and rising to a top marginal rate of 7 percent on income above $7,462,687.[21] This has all changed of course and the tax has increasingly become more punitive and is imposed on far more people. Marginal tax rates today begin at 10 percent with exemptions and deductions that are meager in comparison to the original code. In addition, marginal rates have climbed as high as 91 percent. While they are not that high today, the "soak the rich" mentality that tends to drive discussions of changes in the tax code continues to prevail.

---

[20] Raico, op. cit., pg. 9.
[21] Raymond J. Keating, "Original Intent and the Income Tax," *Ideas on Liberty*, February 1996, pp. 70-71.

While the federal government retrenched somewhat after World War I, there was, nevertheless, a large residue of government activity that remained. Moreover, while the economy advanced in the 1920s, a goodly amount of the growth was financed with artificial credit that had been introduced by the newly created Federal Reserve. This served to promote an economic bubble of expansion that could not be maintained.[22] The day of reckoning arrived in 1929 with a sizable drop in the value of the stock market and the onset of a recessionary economy. The Great Depression that followed marked another opportunity for political leaders to obfuscate the issues, to mislead people generally, and to expand their power and control. No one was better at this than Franklin Delano Roosevelt.

Roosevelt surrounded himself with various social reformers, communist sympathizers, and corporate statists. He came to power during the midst of extreme hardship by arguing persuasively that the incumbent president, Herbert Hoover, was largely to blame for the economic situation the nation faced. Of course, government bungling was to blame for much of the hardship, but Roosevelt certainly had no intention of easing those burdens. For FDR everything was both black and white in the same relationship and at the same time. His world was one of contradictions and inconsistencies that twisted the truth beyond all recognition. On one hand, he called for spending restraint to get government's fiscal house in order and in the next breath he was promoting various grand new governmental schemes that required huge new sources of revenue. In this, he was either delusional, a liar, or some combination of the two. The last of these is most likely the case. Roosevelt was not known for being particularly bright and he probably believed in what he was doing. Nevertheless, he was also politically astute in the Machiavellian sense. In this case, fiscal responsibility was never really pursued but the statement was politically useful and allowed him cover to pursue what he wanted all along. Mainly,

---

[22] Murray N. Rothbard, *America's Great Depression*, (Princeton, NJ: D. Van Nostrand, 1963).

what he wanted was large and expensive new government programs that were pursued with wild abandon.

In fiscal year 1932, federal government expenditures were just under $4.7 billion on receipts of $1.9 billion. While spending and revenues dropped slightly in 1933, both spending and tax receipts rose sharply in 1934. In that fiscal year, federal spending jumped to just over $6.5 billion on tax receipts of just under $3 billion. That is, spending rose by nearly $2 billion with an increase in tax revenue of about $1 billion. In percentage terms, spending increased in that single year by 42 percent and tax receipts increased by 48 percent.[23] Quite contrary to Roosevelt's rhetoric, his actual policies were financially irresponsible. In the end, these new programs extended the power and activity of the federal government in every way imaginable and cost the nation mightily as they insured the continuation of the economic recession for a decade.

Among some of the worst offenses of Roosevelt's New Deal programs were his confiscation of the public's gold and his inflationary monetary policy, his cartelization of agriculture through the Agricultural Adjustment Act, his introduction of fascism via the National Recovery Act, his establishment of Social Security for retirement, which continues to operate as the largest pyramid scheme in human history, and his pandering to the monopolization of labor via his National Labor Relations Act and his Fair Labor Standards Act. These acts brought government involvement and bureaucracy to virtually every area of American life and established a command and control system unimaginable by the nation's founders.

While some of the provisions of these pieces of legislation were initially ruled unconstitutional, they set the stage for what was to come in America. That is, an increasingly meddlesome government populated by people who believe they are better informed about the issues of life than are their

---

[23] United States of America, *Historical Tables: Budget of the United States Government Fiscal Year 2004*, pg. 21, available at www.whitehouse.gov/omb.

neighbors. As a result, they have little respect for their neighbors or for their private rights. Each new administration following that of Roosevelt has felt free to pursue any number of new programs that further usurp the rights of the people to act for themselves. Of course such meddling requires huge amounts of both spending and taxing and those have been readily increased along the way.

> The shift from personal autonomy to dependence on government is perhaps the defining characteristic of modern American politics...Nominal private ownership with largely unlimited government authority to control remains the prevalent politico-economic system at the dawn of the twenty-first century in America. Virtually anything of significance any of us endeavors to accomplish now triggers the application of a plethora of federal rules and policies. Private land use, water use, banking, international trade, science, technology, education, health care, broadcasting, retirement—all and more are bound in a cocoon of federal regulations.[24]

In fiscal year 2002 alone, the federal government's official registry numbered 75,606 pages. Its agencies issued 4,167 new final rules and Congress passed 269 new laws.[25] In 1940, prior to the war, Roosevelt's administration spent $9.5 billion. In 2002, that spending figure had increased to $2,011 billion. In constant 1996 dollars, this would have been the equivalent of spending $94.3 billion in 1940 compared to $1,798 billion in 2002 or a 1,800 percent real increase in federal government outlays.[26] The growth in spending has been so substantial that it is an impossibility that anyone knows all that our government is doing. There is simply no way for even the most informed among

---

[24] Charlotte A. Twight, *Dependent on D. C.: The Rise of Federal Control Over the Lives of Ordinary Americans*, (New York: Palgrave, 2002), pp 1 and 5.
[25] Crews, op. cit.
[26] OMB, op. cit.

us to know what is going on in the quagmire that has been created by political activists since the Roosevelt era. Even the president who presumably oversees the whole mess could not be fully informed about all that goes on in the federal government. Moreover, if the president does not know, the average person does not even understand the tip of the iceberg.

In the discussion of fiscal policy to this point, no mention has been made of budget deficits and the national debt. While it might be an opportune time to take up this examination, it is actually a better time to make a transition to the examination of monetary policy because the two are inevitably linked. Until the Great Depression, the dominant view among economists was that the free market was self-correcting. J. B. Say, a French economist, had done a marvelous job of explaining how a free market functions. In his treatise Say argued that all people who rely upon trade to meet their ends are both consumers and producers. In fact, it is their desire to consume that motivates them to produce. However, if one is to successfully trade with others, he must first produce something that others actually want. There is simply no value in laboring to produce a good that has little value to others. As Say saw the matter, profits and losses by producers would direct their efforts. While it was possible for an entrepreneur to err and produce more of something than warranted by economic realities, the losses incurred would quickly lead him to redirect his resource usage. Thus, market prices would keep the economy moving ahead and lead to greater coordination of human activities and there would be no generalized overproduction in a market economy that was left alone from government meddling and price fixing.[27]

The Depression, which was worldwide, provided an opportunity to propose a new theory that suggested that Say's Law was not true and that in fact the market economy was inherently unstable. John Maynard Keynes seized upon that

---

[27] Peter Anderson, "Say's Law in Context," *Daily Articles*, (Auburn, AL: Mises Institute, July 9, 2003).

opportunity and proposed what came to be the dominant view of the economy since that time. Keynes' thesis was widely embraced by both politicians and economists alike, though it seems strange that economists were so enamored with it. In hindsight, what he did was to set back economic thought by greatly confusing the issue.[28] He revived numerous fallacies and half-truths to concoct a theory that suited his own political leanings.

By the time Keynes wrote his *General Theory*, he had embraced the collectivist spirit of his day. He had become a member of the Fabian Society in England whose primary objective was to promote gradual socialism through public policy initiatives. He was also a member of the aristocratic elite whose families had historically enjoyed positions of political privilege. Thus, it is probably not surprising that he would come up with a rationale why laissez-faire policies were misguided and why they should be replaced by the older command and control institutions that had been practiced beforehand. The new government meddling that had taken place earlier in the century had led to various misallocations in capital that gave rise to the recession of the early thirties. In turn, government officials piled on so to speak by adding new layers of political control thus hindering economic recovery. Was there ever a better time to propose that the economic hardships being experienced were the result of too much economic freedom rather than growing governmental interferences?

It is easy to see why political activists readily welcomed Keynes' analysis of the situation. It offered them something else to blame so that they did not have to recognize their own culpability in the matter. At any rate, Keynes' argument went as follows. The problem with the economy was essentially that there was too little spending or demand. Put another way, too many people were trying to save too much money by hoarding it and this was causing all the problems. According to Keynes, there is a

---

[28] Henry Hazlitt, *The Failure of the 'New Economics': An Analysis of the Keynesian Fallacies*, (Princeton, NJ: D. Van Nostrand, 1959).

"paradox of thrift" that is active in the economy such that when people try to autonomously increase their savings, it reduces aggregate demand which in turn reduces national income and results in a recession. That is, the problem is that people simply cannot be trusted to act rightly when they are allowed to act freely. What is needed in the Keynesian view is some policy aimed at increasing aggregate demand by short circuiting the desires of the market participants themselves.

If ever there were a perverted economic theory, this is it. What Keynes argued essentially is that prodigality is actually a virtue rather than a vice. On his terms, in Jesus' story of the lost son who squandered his inheritance in riotous living, the son's actions are to be seen as wholly just and good. In Keynesian terms his spendthrift tendencies benefited not only the economy, but also himself. What Keynes basically said is that the boy had no reason to ask his father for forgiveness. Rather, it was the father who saved and invested in capital to build a family business that needed to be forgiven because everyone would have been infinitely better off if he had never saved a penny. But, one wonders where in the world the resources ever come from to provide the capital that can be used to produce the goods that are to be consumed in the first place? I suppose that we are expected to assume that slopping pigs for a living is paradise. Keynes never addresses the issue because he simply has no capital theory to speak of. In his world, capital simply drops from the sky as a given. The amount that falls is all that matters and it can be brought about by an unlimited expansion of bank credit. As for government spending, he just assumed that surpluses would be the norm in good times and deficits in those that are bad while his apostles evidently advocate deficits on all occasions.[29] Keynes failed to understand that the act of saving is the act of postponing present consumption from today for some future time and provides the financial wherewithal to accumulate

---

[29] James M. Buchanan and Richard W. Wagner, *Democracy in Deficit*, (New York: Academic Press, 1977).

capital in a modern economy. Keynes entire case is built around the assumption that prices are not flexible enough to bring about economic coordination. But, why would that be the case? Of course the government could have already engaged in various price fixing strategies and, thus, created a situation in which there would be an ongoing disequilibrium in the market. However, if this is the case, it is clearly not the free market that is to be faulted for the economic hardship, but government action. Indeed, this is precisely what happened in the 1930s.

It is easy to see why Keynes' story was readily welcomed by political figures. They had a vested interest in it for it allowed them new opportunities for demagoguery. However, Keynes' story was also accepted widely by economists who should have known better. While not all economists jumped on the Keynesian bandwagon, enough did to make it the dominant explanation of economic matters for quite a long time. Even today, there are staunch defenders of Keynes' theory among the rank and file in the discipline. Why is this true?

There are perhaps several possible explanations. One would be that economists joined support for the new theory because it opened up new job opportunities for them in government service. In an age when more and more resources were being controlled by the government, such political entrepreneurship would enhance one's own financial position even if it were gained through rent seeking. Another possibility is that many economists had already been influenced by socialist ideology and that Keynes' theory fit into their misguided worldview. Perhaps it was just the combination of these two things. Whatever the case, the majority support for Keynesianism meant the abandonment of many sound economic principles that had been learned in the previous two centuries. As a result, economic understanding has been greatly clouded and confused in our time.

Chapter 3: Monetary Policy

Money, Banking, and the Development of Monetary Policy

The development of monetary policy is also important in understanding the big picture of the changing American landscape. Therefore, the purpose of this chapter is to examine the evolution of that policy. Once this is done, the ongoing link between both fiscal and monetary policy can be made as they affect one another in the modern political arena. Of particular importance in this effort will be an examination of how these policies are associated with deficit spending and the growing national debt. These issues will be the focus of this chapter.

In terms of monetary policy, banking and monetary issues have always been regulated in some way in America. In other words, there has never been a time in U.S. history when banks were completely free from political influence and control.[30] From the start, state governments instituted various kinds of restrictions that limited the things that private banks could do. States tended to charter banks as a means for facilitating their own financial needs. The extent of these regulations varied depending on the time and place, but nevertheless kept the banking system from operating freely. As Rothbard pointed out, there are some essential features that would be a part of free market banking. These include the free entry and exit of banking firms into and out of the industry, the absence of subsidies and restrictions on operations, and the forced bankruptcy and liquidation of any bank failing to make good on the promised redemption of its notes.[31] Since these conditions never really existed in the nation's banking industry, it was not free in the

---

[30] For a good history of banking see George A. Selgin, *The Theory of Free Banking: Money Supply Under Competitive Note Issue*, (Totowa, NJ: Rowman & Littlefield, 1988) or Murray Rothbard, *The Mystery of Banking*, (Richardson & Snyder, 1983).
[31] Ibid, pg 216.

strict sense of the term. Hence, the nation's monetary system has always been subject to some form of government control.

On the national level, Alexander Hamilton was among those who advocated federal intervention in the system by favoring the establishment of a national bank. As we have already seen from his mercantilistic tendencies discussed in the previous chapter, his call for such a bank fit well with what he conceived to be the purpose of government. Some national involvement was already assumed given that the Constitution recognized the power of the federal government to coin money. This provision provided a means by which the federal government could establish a standard monetary unit by coining gold and silver in particular weights.[32] The effect of this provision was to remove from the market place the opportunity for standards to evolve according to the desires and actions of market participants.

The national bank that Hamilton had in mind was not a central bank per se. Rather he thought it would operate "both as a private commercial bank and as a public (or national) bank."[33] Thus, he envisioned a bank that would standardize the nation's currency via its issuance of notes, provide credit to the federal government, and serve as an agent of the U.S. Treasury. In this sense, such a bank's stated purpose was not to control the money supply. Nevertheless, it would serve to take the lead position in domestic commercial banking via its privileged position and could use that position to expand the money supply by instituting an easy credit policy. In 1791, Congress passed legislation that established this kind of bank.

From 1791 to 1811, the First Bank of the United States operated as the federal government's bank. Its creation supported a rapid increase in governmental borrowing. By 1796, the bank held $8.2 million in government debt. In turn, monetary expansion pyramided as new banks were established

---

[32] Richard H. Timberlake, *Monetary Policy in the United States: An Intellectual and Institutional History,* (Chicago, IL: The University of Chicago Press, 1978).
[33] Ibid, pg 9.

around the country and used the national bank's new paper as a
basis for their own operations. There remained the Jeffersonian
Republicans who opposed the national bank and aimed to sunset
it after its initial charter expired. Indeed, that is what happened
as political support for the extension of the bank's charter fell
just short.[34]

Nevertheless, regional banks got in on the action by
expanding the issuance of their own notes to purchase new debt
which was sold to finance the War of 1812. The process rapidly
expanded the money supply which led to a banking crisis when
the more conservative banks in the nation attempted the mass
redemption of outstanding bank notes for the gold and silver
which were supposed to lie behind the paper. Since the issuers
were largely unable to make good on their promises of
redemption, a crisis ensued. Rather than allowing the more
liberal note issuing banks to fail, various state governments
intervened and granted to them the special privilege of
suspending payment. This policy set in motion the prospect of an
ongoing monetary inflation in the nation. These episodes
periodically plagued the country and gave rise to economic
booms and busts. At any rate, the suspension of payment on
bank notes led immediately to monetary deflation that resulted
in an economic recession and this, in turn, resulted in renewed
support to re-establish a national bank. This new bank became
known as the Second Bank of the United States.[35]

The Second Bank was chartered in 1816 and was
patterned after the First Bank. In effect, the promoters of this
bank argued that the way out of the monetary crisis that resulted
from easy money was more easy money. Over the next few years
the bank continued to expand the nation's money supply via new
credit. The process of inflation eventually resulted in a panic and
recession that began in 1819 and lasted until 1821. This event
gave hard money advocates additional political ammunition

---

[34] Murray N. Rothbard, *The Mystery of Banking*, (Richardson & Snyder, 1983), pp. 196-197.
[35] Ibid.

which they used effectively. When Andrew Jackson was elected president, he began to promote and implement policies aimed at shoring up the nation's money supply. Among his goals was an effort to put the federal government's finances on a hard money or specie (silver or gold) basis. This was eventually accomplished and served to promote a greater degree of free banking from the 1830s up to the Civil War. Nevertheless, monetary inflation continued periodically since banks operated under the assumption that should a panic arise, they would be allowed to suspend the redemption of their notes. That assumption proved to be generally true. This, coupled with the inflow of silver from Mexico in the 1830s, led to monetary crises in 1837, 1839, and 1857.[36]

The rise of the fortunes of the Whig-Republican party, with its mercantilistic tendencies, brought about a marked change in the hard money policy. Lincoln immediately suspended the practice after his election in 1860. As has already been stated, Lincoln was a devotee of Henry Clay and supported the notion that a strong central government was needed to promote the interests of business. This, along with the slavery issue, led to the split in the country between the North and the South. To fund his war effort against the South he began the process of issuing paper currency, known as greenbacks. This effectively meant that the national government adopted a highly inflationary policy via a fiat monetary system. "The money supply of the country totaled $745 million in 1860; by 1863, the money supply had zoomed to $1.44 billion, an increase of 92.5% in three years, or 30.8% per annum."[37] The whole affair was primarily an effort to establish a system of privilege for certain business interests. In waging the war, slavery served as a useful political tool. The monetary policy was, thus, designed to work in conjunction with the administration's fiscal policy.

Once again, we find that the Lincoln administration

---

[36] Ibid.
[37] Ibid, pp. 221-222.

marked a change in direction that was more or less permanent. What Lincoln did was to crack the door of interventionism open in such a way that it would never be shut again. The ongoing monetary issues that arose from that time on eventually led to centralized banking with the establishment of the Federal Reserve System in 1913. From the end of the Civil War until this time, the American landscape was changing in some profound ways and these eventually led to the consolidation of power and control over money. The latter part of the nineteenth century was marked by the spread of new ideas. Intellectuals and various social reformers of the day began promoting collectivist notions of society that aimed to displace the prevailing individualism that had long been the hallmark of the American order. Interventionist policies that tended to undercut the natural rights of the citizens of that age resulted in various unintended consequences that in turn resulted in new calls among reformers for greater control.[38] One of the culminating points of change of this process was the year 1913. In that year the Constitution was amended to allow for the establishment of an income tax as well as the legislation that created the Federal Reserve. The combination of these two changes drastically altered the nature of American government and its activities.

The creation of the Federal Reserve served to monopolize banking in the United States and put it under government control. This created the situation in which the nation's money supply was controlled by the actions of the Fed. Through its use of the well known tools of monetary policy: its setting of reserve requirements and the discount rate, coupled with its open market operations; the Fed was able to expand or contract the supply of money. An expansion of base money could thus be pyramided in the system via fractional reserve banking.

The Fed was begun with reserves of gold and Treasury

---

[38] For an excellent discussion of the changing mindset of that age see Clarence Carson, *The Fateful Turn: From Individualism to Collectivism 1880-1960*, (Irvington-on-Hudson, NY: Foundation for Economic Education, 1963).

gold notes that were issued on a 100 percent reserve basis. However, after its establishment it departed from that standard and operated on a fractional reserve basis. As a result of these practices, it orchestrated several monetary expansions. The first was primarily driven by the government's need to finance its efforts in World War I. Other monetary expansions took place during the 1920s. The last of these expansions resulted in a large amount of speculation and margin trading in the stock market that gave rise to a sharp increase in security prices. In addition, the easy credit policies of the Fed provided the liquidity for the adoption of new technologies at a rate far faster than would have been possible in a sound money environment. As a result, far more resources were devoted to productive efforts associated with the use of these new technologies than was warranted by the underlying economic realities. This was especially true in the production and implementation of new equipment associated with the agricultural enterprises.

The stock market bubble burst in 1929 and the underlying economic realities came bursting to the fore. Many farmers and other workers found themselves in difficult economic straits because it was clear that some choices to purchase capital that had been made were not going to succeed. Farmers in particular found themselves on the horns of a dilemma so to speak. While they had adopted new means of production that had expanded output, the prices that could be had for the resulting products they produced were not high enough to cover the costs of production that many of them faced. The resulting economic fallout from this event revealed numerous capital investments that were simply unprofitable and a recession resulted from the sharp monetary deflation that resulted. The interventionist policies of both the Hoover and Roosevelt administrations kept the economy from recovery throughout the 1930s and set in motion the kind of fiscal and monetary policies that have plagued the country ever since.

Debts, Deficits, and Keynesian Economics

As mentioned in the previous chapter, it was during these events that Keynes proposed a new economic understanding of recessions. According to his view, what was needed in the time of a recession was increased spending to raise aggregate demand. This would be accomplished by expanding government spending, by cutting taxes, or by some combination of the two. Moreover, one way (in Keynes' view perhaps the best way) to finance this spending was through monetary expansion. That is, the monetary authorities should intervene by re-inflating the money supply. In the monetary system that had been created this could be accomplished by the Fed making purchases of federal government debt in the open market. The ability of the Fed to do this was greatly enhanced when Roosevelt took the nation off the gold standard early in his first term. He took this action as a supposed emergency response which was needed to deal with the Depression. He confiscated private gold holdings and, thus, introduced a pure fiat monetary system in domestic economic affairs. In this way, an ongoing inflation became a new means of taxing the American citizenry to pay for government programs.

One of the supposed benefits of the Federal Reserve System was that it was theoretically independent of the federal government. However, in practice that has not proven to be entirely true. As DiLorenzo observed,

> In 1935 Franklin D. Roosevelt 'packed' the Fed's board of governors with political hacks just as he would later pack the US Supreme Court. FDR appointed Marriner Eccles as Fed Chairman even though Eccles had no financial background and lacked even a college degree. In reality, the Fed was run by Eccles's political mentor, Treasury Secretary Henry Morganthau, Jr., which is to say, it was run by

Roosevelt."[39]

In Robert Weintraub's article, he discerned marked shifts in Fed policy that were related to political changes.[40] These connections are important since they give evidence that the Fed has generally operated primarily for the benefit of the federal government rather than at the behest of the banking system. At the very least, it can be said that there is an ongoing tension between the interests of government and those of bankers and they are not always identical. While private firms often seek to organize their industries as state run cartels, the banking cartel has not always worked out in the interests of the bankers. Quite the opposite is often true.

This reality can be illustrated by noting that actions which would be good for one business enterprise may well harm another effort. For example, during the latter part of the nineteenth century the government intervened in the railroad business by offering large subsidies of money and land to construct transcontinental roads. Large tracks of government land were given to several firms who were also provided subsidies for every mile of railroad track they laid. As Folsom showed, under these incentives the firms accepting the government aid operated more in the track laying business than in the railroad business.[41] They used low quality, cheap materials to construct their lines, took no thought of grades or distance since any mile laid added to their subsidy, and generally paid no attention to the details necessary for operating a successful railroad after construction was completed. Thereafter, all the transcontinental railroads that had been constructed with government money failed. Only James Hill's Great Northern stretching from Minneapolis-St. Paul to Seattle succeeded. Hill built his railroad entirely with private funds. He succeeded where others failed

---

[39] Thomas J. DiLorenzo, "The Federal Reserve and Political Corruption," *The Free Market*, (Auburn, AL: The Mises Institute, May 2000).

[40] Robert Weintraub, "Congressional Supervision of Monetary Policy," *Journal of Monetary Economics*, April 1978, 341-362.

[41] Burton W. Folsom, *The Myth of the Robber Barons*, (Herndon, VA: Young America's Foundation, 1991).

because he understood clearly that he was in the railroad business and built his line for that purpose.

The banking business can be the same way. One of the chief problems associated with fractional reserve banking is that it is tantamount to counterfeiting. The counterfeiting enterprise can certainly be lucrative however it is at odds with the banking business. Counterfeit money succeeds in the market because it captures the value of resources by reducing the value of money itself. That is, the counterfeiter is able to steal the wealth of others by way of fraud. The better the representation of money the counterfeiter makes, the better able he is in purchasing resources and executing his crime. Those individuals from whom resources have been stolen are those who receive the counterfeit money late in the process of exchange and those who never receive it at all. They lose because the value of their money holdings is eroded.

It is for this reason that governments have historically wanted to control money. Throughout history there are examples of governments and various other rulers who have used the control of money to capture resources for their own use. There are a multitude of examples of rulers debasing the coinage or issuing paper currency far beyond their governments' ability to redeem the notes. The attractiveness of this kind of state finance is easy to see. The ruler can tax his citizens without tax collectors.

The material gains from inflation of this sort are also beneficial to those who are able to get their hands on the new money first. In this context one can understand the attraction that bankers might have for it. They may make significant gains by what they are able to purchase with the new money before its value is depressed. However, the banking business itself can suffer greatly from counterfeiting to the extent that it involves the borrowing and lending of money. In fact, it is always the borrowers who gain most from unforeseen inflation at the expense of the lenders. For this reason, the monetary system in place in America operates in a more or less schizophrenic fashion as the competing interests of those involved attempt to direct the system to their greatest benefit. Moreover, it appears that this has been what has been going on for some time as politically promoted monetary inflation eventually gives way to a deflationary bust that results in bank failures and in short term reversions to sounder money which eventually gives way to new rounds of inflation.

Since the end of the Roosevelt administration, and the end of World War II, the federal government of the United States has continued to expand both its size and scope. Sometimes the increase is rapid and other times it is slower. But, it has increased nonetheless. The combination of the prevailing Keynesian ideas about the economy, coupled with the ideological shift in understanding about the purpose of government, has aided this process of change. This was especially true beginning in the 1960s. At that time, the federal government embarked on an excess spending spree as it began to run regular budget deficits. To finance the excess, political pressure was imposed on Fed officials to monetize the debt to keep interest rates low. During that decade, spending jumped 52% and the nation's debt rose 31%. The combination of these monetary and fiscal policies resulted in a boom and bust cycle which culminated with a recession in the early 1970s. This kind of maneuvering has continued on ever since. It has resulted in periodic booms and busts and in a growing national debt coupled with the declining value of the dollar. The nation has been shielded in the most recent decade from the detrimental effects of the latter problem due to the privileged position the dollar maintains in world trade. In short, the nation has been able to largely export its inflation and, thereby impose the cost of it onto other people around the world.

The figures associated with this understanding are telling. In real terms (1996 dollars), government expenditures rose from $493 billion in 1950 to $1,660.6 billion in 2000. This represents a 431% increase in the real size of government in the last half of the twentieth century. The nation's debt increased in that same period from $256 billion to $5,269 billion or a 1,958% increase

in debt load of the federal government.[42] These numbers do not
include spending in so called off budget programs, nor the
indebtedness of the Social Security program, nor the costs of
federal mandates to states. All told, the combination of fiat
money and the ability to inflate at will coupled with the
prevailing ideological currents has led to the creation of
Leviathan.

---

[42] United States of America, Historical Tables: Budget of the United States Government Fiscal Year 2004,
available at www.whitehouse.gov/omb.

Chapter 4: Transportation Policy

Introduction

Trade has always been fundamental to the advancement of human well being and transportation has always been one of the chief obstacles that human beings have had to overcome to engage in trade. The desire and need for mobility is an integral factor that must be considered in any human undertaking. Indeed, the development and spread of new and more efficient means of transportation has been a significant factor that helps to explain an improvement in the economic circumstances that people face.

The modes of transportation that have been used include those designed for water, land, and air transport. Of course, the last of these is a more recent development. Nonetheless, the improvements made in each of these means of transportation have served to reduce the cost of trade which has resulted in its expansion and increased economic progress. Therefore, a consideration of transportation policies will be important to any economic history of public policy.

Water and Railroad Transportation

From the beginning of recorded human history, waterways have been the main mode of transportation used for hauling large amounts of cargo long distances. The reason for this is that it was, and still is, the cheapest means of hauling large quantities of goods. This fact was certainly true in the early development of America which led to the establishment of port cities as the main trading and commercial centers. Americans made use of the various waterways within their territories by designing water craft suitable for each situation in the conveyance of goods and the transport of people. Such transportation was greatly aided by the development of the steam engine and the invention of the steamboat in 1807. Robert Fulton is often credited with the invention, though others were working on similar projects. Whatever the case, the steamboat dramatically improved river travel because it solved the problem of going against the current.

In Fulton's invention and use of the steamboat we have an example of the difference between what Burton Folsom referred to as political entrepreneurship versus market entrepreneurship.[43] In his historical analysis, Folsom showed that Fulton acted as a political entrepreneur against the market entrepreneurial behavior of Cornelius Vanderbilt. From the outset, Fulton aimed to take advantage of his invention with the aid of the State of New York which granted him the monopoly right of transportation on the Hudson River. Vanderbilt was hired by another steamboat company to challenge that political privilege. Since this company operated out of New Jersey, it maintained that New York's law did not apply and that the company was free to compete for passengers trafficking along the Hudson River. The case was tried in the judicial system and eventually made its way to the Supreme Court of the United States where the Fulton monopoly was struck down in the case of *Gibbons v. Ogden*. This decision provided a decided edge for market entrepreneurship for years to come as it held political entrepreneurship at bay by affirming the rights of sellers thus supporting market competition.

Beyond the issue of government granted monopoly rights, one of the chief drawbacks of water transportation is that it is limited to available navigable waterways. This geographical problem imposed limitations on the kinds of transportation that were feasible. These limitations coupled with the political competition between communities at the time led to the construction of numerous canals aimed at linking various bodies

---

[43] Burton W. Folsom, Jr., *The Myth of the Robber Barons: A New Look at the Rise of Big Business in America*, (Herndon, VA: Young America's Foundation, 2003, 4th edition).

of water. These canals were largely built with state money along with some private financing. While some of the canals built in this era were very successful, many turned out to be a waste of money. Such wastes tended to reveal a fundamental principle in public choice literature. Namely, politicians are more likely to risk taxpayers' money for all kinds of projects that private investors would never contemplate because of the likely losses that would result. As such, political figures and bureaucrats are likely to squander scarce capital assets.

Despite this principle, the most famous of the canals built, the Erie Canal in the state of New York, turned out to be very successful. In fact, its success spurred other state and local governments to fund the construction of many unsuccessful ventures. It stretched from Buffalo in western New York to the Hudson River at Troy. Thus, it served to link New York City to the Midwest via the Great Lakes. In fact, the impetus for constructing the canal initially was to maintain New York City's dominance as a port city by drawing traffic away from the Mississippi River. Of course this project did not draw all the traffic in that direction, but it did draw a significant proportion of it. Despite its success, the canal was eventually abandoned as an avenue of conveyance because of the shifting nature of transport services.

In addition to the problem of availability of navigable waterways, water transportation is limited by climatic conditions. Indeed, during the winter months the Erie Canal was impassible. Therefore, its use was limited to seven months out of the year.[44] For this reason, railroad transportation provided significant advantages even though it was generally a little more costly. First, such transportation provided a more dependable operating schedule which could be met year round. In addition, it had greater flexibility and could be operated between any particular locations as long as a suitable rail line could be constructed.

---

[44] Clarence B. Carson, *A Basic History of the United States Volume 3: The Sections and the Civil War 1826-1877*, (Phenix City, AL: The American Textbook Committee, 1985), pg. 107.

With the invention of the steam locomotive in 1829, the amount of capital investment in railroads began to increase. While such investments could be entirely made by private investors, once again state and local governments often intervened and subsidized the effort. As was the case with the building of canals, once again taxpayers were often left liable for poor investment decisions. Such financial failures tended to hold in check the amount of public funds diverted to such projects. Nonetheless, public subsidies for rail line construction remained sizable.

Beyond state and local funding of the railways, there was also a push for federal financing. Such efforts were largely unsuccessful during the early to mid 1800s when the Jacksonian Democrats controlled the political landscape of America. However, as the influence and political power of the Whig Party (and later the Republicans) advanced, so too did the appeal for federal funding of such business ventures. Once again, the election of Lincoln in 1860 marked a watershed of shorts. In 1862, Congress passed two pieces of legislation that profoundly affected the nature of American economic development. First, it passed the Homestead Act which made land available at nearly no cost to people willing to develop it. Second, it passed the Pacific Railway Act which initiated the federal government's involvement in promoting the development of transcontinental railways. Combined with subsequent legislation, the federal government entered into the promotion of the railroad business by providing large grants of land and low cost loans for railroad construction. The loans made available varied from $16,000 to $48,000 per mile constructed depending on the terrain.[45] The combination of this legislation provided for the rapid development of the western region of the United States. It also provided ample opportunity for numerous political entrepreneurs to take advantage of the situation.

For example, historian Burton Folsom recounted the

---

[45] D. Philip Locklin, *Economics of Transportation*, (Homewood, IL: Richard D. Irwin, Inc., 1966, 6th edition), pg. 107.

activities of the Union Pacific and the Central Pacific as they took advantage of the government's largess.[46] Folsom explained well the strategy both railroads pursued in constructing their lines. Namely, both firms were more interested in obtaining the government land grants and loans than they were in operating successful railroads. As a result, they did not concern themselves with issues that would be important to operating efficient railroad lines. Rather, they used the cheapest possible materials and laid track on the most circuitous routes in an effort to obtain the most land and the largest amounts of monetary loans possible by laying as many miles of track as possible. After their completion, these railroads were ill prepared to provide efficient service. In addition, in many cases the demand for their services was so sparse that the railroads had to launch new programs to entice people to the west with offers of cheap land. There were many willing takers of these offers as numerous immigrants were eager to have their own homes. They traveled west to enter into various agricultural enterprises. However, as will be discussed more fully in the next chapter on agricultural policy, the increase in output resulting from the rapid expansion in farming, coupled with the advances in technology used in farming, depressed farm product prices and undercut marginal and sub-marginal farmers. As a result, the poorest farmers in both the east and the west suffered heavy losses and were forced to abandon farming altogether.

Beyond the problems encountered by the new farmers, cases of corruption in the railroad industry began to be exposed. Such corruption typically follows the offer of government money for business enterprise and America's experience in subsidizing the railroads was no different. The railroads that were making their living off government money readily courted politicians and bureaucrats in order to maintain and advance their political privilege. In addition, the monetary giveaways offered plenty of opportunity for those so inclined to grab all they could get by way

---

[46] Folsom, op. cit., pp. 17-39.

of fraud. The combination of the hardships incurred by farmers generally, coupled with the high transportation rates that the railroads charged and the accusations of fraud and corruption, led to calls for the federal government to regulate the industry.

Among the complaints raised by farmers was the claim that the railroads were price discriminating. That is, that they were charging different prices to different customers for the same basic service. The charge arose as some farmers realized that the rates quoted to them for rail service might be quite a bit higher than those quoted to farmers in some other communities which were relatively close to their own. Certainly this was the case, and in the eyes of the farmers this amounted to an injustice.

But this claim largely fails to be meaningful because it misses the bigger economic picture and misunderstands how markets function in practice. To say this, is merely to say that businesses engage in practices aimed at maximizing their profits given the situations they face in any particular markets. That is, businesses engage in all sorts of strategies to extend their profits. "Business organizations compete by differentiating products, innovating new products, discounting list prices, locating in areas convenient to consumers, advertising prices and services, and purchasing resources cheaper than rivals."[47] All of these things were going on in the railroad industry at this time. The main reason for the price disparities was mostly the result of government largess at work. This largess created numerous economic disparities in the various locations that the railroads served. The railroads were merely taking advantage of the opportunities as they presented themselves at the time. The very nature of the market process is that such profit opportunities are eroded over time as competition between firms occurs. In the transportation industry at this time, the price disparities provided strong incentives for market entrepreneurs to enter various markets and to make new offers for service.

---

[47] Dominick T. Armentano, *Antitrust and Monopoly: Anatomy of a Policy Failure*, (New York: John Wiley & Sons, 1982), pg. 27.

Nevertheless, the farmers were suffering and the railroads provided an easy target. The corruption and fraud committed by some provided reasonable evidence that the whole system was unjust. Of course that was not true. Not all of the businessmen involved in the railroad business were acting fraudulently. In fact, one man in particular characterized what must be considered the best of business practices. That man was James Hill who built the only transcontinental railroad using only private funding.[48] When completed, his Great Northern line stretched from St. Paul-Minneapolis to Seattle. Moreover, because every mile of track had been laid with the intention of operating a successful railroad on it, it had been built using the highest quality materials on the best possible route. As a result, it was the only transcontinental line not to go bankrupt. Just the same, Hill, like other railroad operators, became an object of attack.

In essence, what the farmers wanted was to limit the freedom of some people for their own benefit. Put another way, they wanted to usurp the property rights of railroad operators by using the power of government to force them to sell their services at prices that the farmers would prefer. This is not how the free market works. In the free market, both parties are free to negotiate on their own terms and to bargain according to their own pleasure in any given situation. Thus, in a free market, the seller cannot ignore what people will pay voluntarily for his product. In addition, he cannot physically force potential buyers to pay his price. He can only offer his product to possible customers based upon the situation as he sees it. Likewise, the buyer is free to take or leave the product at the price at which it is offered, or to attempt to negotiate a lower price if he can. But, he is not free to compel the seller to sell him the product at a price he is willing to pay. Certainly, everyone would prefer to pay less for the products he buys, but that is just a preference. In the case of price discrimination as it was practiced during this time period, these are the kinds of situations that create the tension

---

[48] Folsom provides the complete details of the story in his book, *Myth of the Robber Barons,* op. cit.

that generally leads to entrepreneurial advancements. That is, they are opportunities for market entrepreneurs to offer new products at better prices. These activities would have eventually reduced transportation costs if they had been allowed to occur. But the farmers were not willing to wait for that kind of competition and sought to gain and employ political privilege instead.

While the response of the farmers is typical in such circumstances, it misses the point. The hardships being incurred were not primarily the result of private enterprise, but rather they were the result of the unintended consequences of earlier government action. Indeed, the government's subsidization of the transcontinental railroads led to the development of the west far faster than private individuals would have done on their own. As a result, numerous capital investments were made that were not economically warranted and others were made that merely offered the opportunity for large short term profits to be reaped. In addition, when governments create this kind of environment, they invite men to grab all the money that might be had and to leave others holding the empty bag of poor capital investments. That is what happened in the case of the railroads in the latter half of the nineteenth century.

The call for greater government involvement in such cases is the most imprudent thing that can be done because it tends to undercut the very market process of competition. Nevertheless, that is what happened. Initially, state legislatures provided regulatory control. Eventually, Congress responded in 1887 by creating the Interstate Commerce Commission (ICC) which was set up to control railroad rates. This legislation advanced the notion that it is the federal government's role in society to regulate commerce and to control the prices at which sellers can sell their products. This was a marked departure from the free market stance that had been the hallmark of the American way of life beforehand. That is not to say that people's lives in America were now largely regulated, because they were not. People were for the most part free to engage in any business activity they wished and to sell the resulting product on terms that were agreeable to them. However, the regulations imposed on the railroad industry set a new tone for government action that grew in size and scope over time.

Once in place, regulation over transportation services was expanded and extended over the years until the mid 1970s. Rates for transportation service were regulated by the ICC which set up a system of elaborate rules that controlled the industry. Beyond simply controlling railroad rates, the regulations were extended to truck and water transportation as well. In time the rules became more cumbersome and perverse. By the late sixties and early seventies, the abundance of such inefficiencies made it clear to many economists that government regulations were merely driving up the general cost of transportation. In the 1970s, economists were making significant arguments in favor of the deregulation of transportation generally. In 1976, Congress moved in this direction by passing the Railroad Revitalization and Regulatory Reform Act. The legislation eliminated some of the more burdensome rules that afflicted the industry. This led to additional legislation, including the Staggers Act and the Motor Carrier Act both of 1980. These further freed the various forms of transportation services in America. The reductions in regulatory control resulted in the sharp reduction in prices and the freeing of the various forms of transportation for more effective market competition.[49] For example, "[b]y 1988 railroad rates had fallen to 2.6 [cents] per ton-mile from 4.2 [cents] per ton-mile in the 1970s."[50] Moreover, the new freedom afforded railroad managers led to greater efficiency and greater profitability for the railroads. Despite the recent success of deregulation, numerous regulatory impediments to a free market in transportation remain in place to this day. These remaining rules continue to hinder the market process of change in the

---

[49] For excellent discussions of the move toward deregulation see Thomas Gale Moore, "Clearing the Track: The Remaining Transportation Regulations," *Regulation*, Spring 1995, or his article, "Rail and Truck Reform: The Record so Far," *Regulation*, Summer 1991.

[50] Moore, 1995, pg. 1.

transportation industry.

Automotive Transportation and the Smart Growth Movement

The invention of the automobile changed the nature of transportation in America. It provided an inexpensive and convenient means of personal transportation that had not existed beforehand. Following Henry Ford's entrepreneurial efforts to produce automobiles at a low per unit cost, car ownership spread rapidly. In addition, trucking provided a new, more flexible, means of hauling goods. As a result, the demand for more and better roadways on which these vehicles could be operated increased. For better or worse, it had always been assumed that the government had a role to play in the construction and maintenance of these roadways. Thus, the increase in the demand for roads initially fell mainly upon state and local governments. The federal government quickly got involved in the process in 1916 when Congress passed the Federal-Aid Road Act. From this initial starting point, federal government involvement increased over the years with its most significant impact being the planning and development of the Interstate Highway system.

Over the years, roads were constructed using several different kinds of funding. For instance, some were constructed with revenue bonds which were to be paid for by way of tolls charged for using the road. Others were constructed using general revenues from the various governments involved. However, as time went by, there was a move for more of the construction and maintenance of the roadways to be funded by gasoline taxes and other user fees. In effect, these taxes linked the construction and maintenance so as to tie the supply of roads with the demand for them since the users would be those who primarily paid for them. Increased demand for more and/or better roads would be obvious as the fuel taxes or other user fees would at the same time generate more revenue. To the extent that road construction and maintenance is funded in this way, the resulting highway system tends to function reasonably well. Indeed, adjusting such user fees can provide a reasonably good system of roadways that allows the users a great deal of freedom of choice. This has more or less been America's general experience. While a purely private road system might have been constructed, and while it might have been superior to the one that we have, that did not happen and it is hard for people to imagine such a situation as a real option today. Just the same, transportation policy can operate relatively efficiently when the payment of projects is linked to user fees because this better coordinates the resource allocations. This is why market economies work well. Namely, markets provide participants with price information that they can use to better manage their own resources. When government intervention short-circuits these links by diverting these user fees to other purposes, the information embedded in prices is lost and resources tend to be more readily squandered.

Table 4.1 provides data for the decade of the 1990s and shows the extent to which each means of transportation was

Table 4.1 The Portion of Governmental Expenditures Financed by User Fees for Each Mode of Transportation					
	1991	1993	1995	1997	1999
Highways	0.857	0.903	0.877	0.9	0.986
Air Transportation	0.853	0.732	0.822	0.721	0.967
Water Transportation	0.486	0.515	0.538	0.529	0.511
Transit	0.27	0.274	0.25	0.276	0.266
Highway Subsidy of Transit*	0.359	0.319	0.301	0.35	0.415

The table was constructed using Bureau of Transportation data as a ratio of revenues received by each mode of transportation divided by the expenses born by government for each mode.

*This line shows the portion of the cost of transit that is paid for by diverting highway user fees.

funded by user fees. As is clear from the data, air transportation and highways are largely funded by such fees and receive very little subsidization from general revenues. As a matter of policy improvement, adjustments could be made to the user fees so that they would cover all expenses incurred. This change in policy would make the link between the users of the projects funded and the supply of those projects stronger and this would be an improvement over the current situation. On the other hand, heavy government subsidization of other modes should be questioned. It is clear from the data in Table 4.1 that water transportation and transit are receiving large scale subsidies and the value of these expenditures ought to be evaluated.

In particular, note that public transit is mainly funded by subsidization. This is significant because rather than moving to strengthen the link between the collection of user fees and the construction of projects, legislators and bureaucrats have actually been working in recent years to destroy that link. In fact, they have been pursuing a course of action aimed at expanding the number of transit projects by siphoning off funds from highway user fees. In the most recent year of data presented in Table 4.1, 41.5% of the total amount spent on public transit was diverted from highway user fees.

This direction in public policy is being driven by the notion that the cities of the nation are sprawling. Some people believe that large cities are growing too large and are spreading out too far. According to their way of thinking, something needs to be done to limit this kind of expansion. As a result, these people are proposing a new urban planning effort that is known generically as the smart growth movement. Advocates of the concept of smart growth include a variety of special interest groups such as bureaucrats, politicians, and environmentalists as well as certain business firms that might profit from the public projects proposed by these new planners. Stated fundamentally, smart growth advocates propose urban plans which would increase the density of the nation's cities by controlling land use. Central to their plans is the construction of mass transportation systems around which other projects would be developed. The goal is to limit the number of private, single family dwellings and to increase the number of multifamily units constructed. According to smart growth advocates, implementing these plans will reduce sprawl which they claim will in turn lead to less traffic congestion, a cleaner environment, and even greater community and civility among people. However, the evidence suggests that just the opposite will actually be achieved.

The growing emphasis on mass transportation is being pursued in spite of the evidence of the tremendous economic success that has come from the spread of private transportation. Smart growth advocates insist on promoting large scale mass transportation projects even though ridership on these modes of transportation has continued to fall as more and more people choose more efficient alternatives, namely the automobile. As one research study observed, "The 10 U.S. cities that added light rail in the years 1980-95 experienced a collective system-wide ridership *loss* of 2 percent."[51] That is, while these cities built these public systems at considerable taxpayer expense, the number of riders continues to fall which means they must be more heavily subsidized in the future if they are to be maintained. Thus, not only did they soak up scarce capital when they were constructed, but they will continue to soak it up if they continue to operate. In truth, the automobile provides a much richer array of transportation services when compared against mass transportation systems which can only offer some rather fixed options for passengers. In fact, a public-transit commuter trip takes about 80 percent longer than one taken by automobile.[52] Thus, it is not at all surprising that the numbers of riders choosing public transportation has been on the decline in an economy where increasing wealth affords more people the wherewithal to choose the more convenient transportation option.

Despite this truth, smart growth advocates continue to rave about light rail transit projects. They argue that at its full volume, a light rail system can carry as many passengers as a six

---

[51] Peter Gordon and Harry Richardson, "Critiquing Sprawl's Critics," Cato Institute Policy Analysis No. 365, January 24, 2000, pg. 8.

[52] Randall O'Toole, "Will Congress Make it Harder for You to Travel?" Cato Institute News Brief, September 30, 1997.

lane freeway. However, no light rail system constructed as a result of the new smart growth efforts operates at full volume. In fact, the average volume carried on the new light rail lines constructed thus far carries eighty percent less volume than a single lane couplet (one lane of freeway highway moving in each direction).[53] What is worse, these projects are terribly expensive. As one researcher found, when considering how much it cost taxpayers to provide the service, in almost every case it would have been cheaper to have leased an economy automobile in perpetuity for each new commuter choosing public transit than to have built the line in the first place. In some cases, it would have been cheaper to lease a luxury automobile such as a BMW 7 series.[54] These facts demonstrate the utter foolishness of the new urban planning efforts. Nonetheless, advocates of more spending along these lines continue to maintain their stance and to push for even grander projects.

Beyond the costs and the lack of ridership, the mass transit projects result in greater traffic congestion, not less. Federal highway dollars that could have been used to expand existing roadways and to build new roadways is steadily being diverted to these projects thus constricting the supply of roads. This will result in greater urban congestion. As a result, it is apparent that the real aim of urban planners is to penalize users of private automobiles.

But, why would policy makers want to penalize people for driving? The answer is that the special interest groups involved in promoting smart growth think that they will benefit in some way or another by imposing such penalties. For example, environmental activists promote smart growth because they believe that the automobile is a significant factor in polluting the air. For them, the automobile is one human invention that needs to be extinct. Therefore, they push for smart growth policies on

[53] Wendell Cox, "Competition, Not Monopolies, Can Improve Public Transit," Heritage Foundation Backgrounder No. 1389, August 1, 2000, pg. 2.
[54] Wendell Cox Consulting, "Urban Rail: Uses and Misuses of Policy Statement," March 2000. Available online at www.publicpurpose.com.

the basis of this belief. The evidence, however, goes against the environmentalists aspirations. One would think that they would actually care about the environment and approach the subject in a rational way that would actually contribute to a better environment. That is not what is happening here. If the smart growth agenda is implemented, the most likely outcome will be greater air pollution. According to the EPAs own data, stop and go traffic produces more air pollution than the same amount of traffic cruising at highway speeds. Thus the push for smart growth will lead to increased traffic congestion which will result in more pollution as cars get stuck for longer periods of time in traffic tie-ups. This fact notwithstanding, the environmentalists continue to press for smart growth policies.

Another special interest group pushing smart growth includes politicians and bureaucrats. They promote these kinds of policies because they tend to produce the kinds of restrictions and controls that would allow them to hold their constituencies captive and force greater dependency on government. Thus they are able to fleece the public for greater amounts of money by imposing higher taxes on them and undertaking ever more public works projects. The corrupt among them are especially excited about this prospect as it would allow them greater opportunity to materially gain by grazing at the public trough. But even the outwardly honest among them are excited about the prospect of being able to plan everyone else's life. In the true sense, politics and government seem to attract those among us who tend to be the most meddlesome people around. They simply do not seem able to mind their own business because of their desire to mind everyone else's for fun and profit.

Finally, it is understandable why some businesses would see these projects as a boon. Anyone who might think he could make a dollar off such plans will be tempted to support smart growth because of the prospect for personal gain. However, to do so is to ignore one of the first caveats of all business activity. Namely, it is better to be in business in an economy where people are wealthy enough to be able to afford to buy my product than in one in which they could not. To the extent that such projects actually undercut the economic progress of the community is the extent to which business supporters of these projects are cutting their own throats. Of course, this is not likely to happen for quite some time, so many ignore this principle now for the quick gain that can be had.

The combination of these interest groups has led to some perverse legislation that tends to undermine the efficiency of the nation's transportation system. The legislation involved includes the Clean Air Act, the Intermodal Surface Transportation Efficiency Act (ISTEA), and the Transportation Efficiency Act for the 21st Century (TEA-21). Under the terms of the Clean Air Act, the EPA has established air quality standards that communities must meet. In the mid 1990s, the EPA made these standards more stringent, thus pushing more communities into noncompliance. Under such circumstances, the EPA was granted the authority to seize a city's highway funding and thus thwart new highway construction. Working with the DOT, the EPA has used this authority to push smart growth policies in cities all over the country. The perversion is that this policy virtually assures a community that it may never meet compliance since it is unable to build a sufficient supply of roadways to handle its traffic well. As the supply of roadways is constricted, congestion increases, pollution rises and the city violates the clean air standards more often. Not only that, but the DOT and EPA are using federal funds to extend grants to organizations that will push for more smart growth policies. The aim of the bureaucrats is not to reduce air pollution, but to expand their own power and control.

At its core, the smart growth movement is an exercise in social engineering founded on a collectivist, utopian philosophy. As one writer put it, the movement is an anti-opportunity movement because it forces housing prices and transportation costs up. This harms the poor most since they are least able to pay the new higher prices.[55] In truth, "when smart-growth

[55] Wendell Cox Consulting, "The Opiate of the Planners: Smart Growth and Urban Containment," The

planners say they want to give people choices, they mean they want to take choices away. When they say they want to relieve congestion, they mean they want to increase congestion so that people will be forced to ride transit. When they say they want affordable housing, they mean they want to make single-family housing unaffordable so that all but the wealthiest people will live in high-density housing. When they say they want to preserve open spaces for people, they mean they want to preserve it *from* people."[56]

The fact of the matter is that some cities are growing larger because more people are moving from rural areas to them. This has occurred because technological advancements made in farming mean that fewer people are needed in agricultural pursuits. As a result, the focus of commercial activity has shifted to the cities. Sprawl is the means by which people make the most of the opportunities that they see before them as it allows them to achieve the highest quality of their lives. The development of suburban America was the result of numerous desires on the part of the people who developed these communities. Among these is the desire to live in less polluted environments, the desire to provide children with better educational opportunities, the desire to avoid becoming the victim of crime, the desire to obtain a degree of personal privacy, and the desire to avoid the higher taxes and ample corruption typically associated with large city governments. While cities have grown, the use of surrounding land is not nearly as great as the amount of land that has been taken out of agricultural production in the country. Indeed, only three percent of the nation is urbanized. The remaining ninety-seven percent is rural.[57]

Public Purpose Commentary, No. 70, August 2003.

[56] Randall O'Toole, *The Vanishing Automobile and Other Urban Myths*, (Bandon, Oregon: The Thoreau Institute, 2001), pg. 8.

[57] Cox, August 2003, op. cit.

Air Transportation

The air transportation industry began in 1925 when Congress passed the Kelly Act, which authorized the United States Post Office to contract with private carriers for airmail delivery. The transportation service offered at that time was merely the hauling of mail. Thus, the industry began its operations relying on government contracts. The carriage of paying passengers came later and was initially thought of as merely a means of extending revenues by adding an additional service to the already established business. In time, the process of awarding the mail contracts was contested and this eventually led to the Civil Aeronautics Act of 1938. This legislation established the Civil Aeronautics Board (CAB).[58]

The CAB was given the authority to control entry and exit into city-pair markets and to set prices for service. In addition, the CAB was charged with the task of promoting safety in air travel. It was in this regulatory environment that the air transportation industry originally developed. The CAB, thus, oversaw the industry, which became dominated by a few large firms that were awarded the right to fly most of the larger routes. The larger airlines, known at the time as trunk carriers, became national in scope. In addition, there were a number of smaller airlines that served markets that were considered too small for these larger airlines to bother with.

Despite the regulatory control, the industry expanded as new aircraft were developed and put into service. As these technological innovations were being made, the passenger service side of the business grew. In time, passenger transportation became the main business of the airlines, though they continued to carry mail. In addition, in 1958, the authority to oversee air travel safety was taken away from the CAB and given to the newly created Federal Aviation Administration (FAA).

---

[58] For a longer history of airline regulation see, Paul A. Cleveland, "Domestic Trunk Air Transportation: From Regulatory Control to Deregulation," *Essays in Economic and Business History*, Volume VII, 1989, pp. 176-189.

In essence, the government ran the industry as a rather large government cartel. While the airlines did compete in some ways, they did not compete in price and could not enter a market unless the CAB granted them permission to do so. As a result, prices for air travel remained higher than they would have been otherwise. The profits from such an arrangement were captured by the airline employees and were eroded away by various forms of non-price competition among the airlines.

In the early 1970s, numerous economists and other policy experts began to question the wisdom of CAB regulation. In their view, the case for regulation was weak and there was abundant evidence that prices were being held far above what would prevail in airline markets if the companies were free to set their own rates. One example of this evidence was the founding of Southwest Airlines. Southwest began solely as an intrastate airline operating only in city-pair markets in the state of Texas. Since the airline did not cross state lines in the course of doing business, it avoided CAB control. One of its major routes was the Dallas/Houston market, which was one of the five busiest markets in the U.S. Southwest was offering to provide passenger service on this route for about half the price that was mandated by the regulators.

In the latter half of the 70s, President Carter appointed Alfred Kahn as chairman of the CAB. Kahn was an economist sympathetic to the case for deregulation. As a result, he carried out his regulatory duties in a much more relaxed way compared to those who went before him. In essence, he allowed the airlines a far greater degree of freedom to set prices and enter markets than they had ever had beforehand. In addition, the push was being made legislatively to decontrol the industry. That legislation was passed in 1978. It laid out a plan by which CAB regulation was to be eliminated. This set in motion a surge of competition in the airline industry that has resulted in falling prices and the rapid increase in air travel.

Since deregulation, there has been a significant amount of competition among the airlines. As would be expected, some airlines were not prepared for this competition and failed as a result of it. In addition, there have been numerous new ventures. Some have succeeded and others have failed and some have been purchased or merged with other firms. In real terms, airfares substantially dropped. As a result, passenger traffic increased dramatically. Today, more people fly more places than ever before.

Some of the main problems in air travel today stem from the fact that air safety and air traffic control remain in the hands of federal bureaucrats.[59] One of the most significant of these problems is the high level of congestion at major airports. This results in numerous flight delays, which imposes a great deal of inconvenience on the traveling public. While the technology exists to develop a more efficient GPS system for air traffic control, the federal authorities have been exceedingly slow to develop it. Astoundingly, this is true in spite of the fact that all commercial aircraft are equipped with such a location system. The main reason for the holdup is that government officials do not realize the costs of their failure to act and, thus, have no incentive to act as rapidly as private decision makers in regards to such new technology. Put simply, the main problem with air transportation today is the failure to completely decontrol the industry by eliminating the FAA and other agency controls.

---

[59] For a complete analysis of FAA regulation see, Paul A. Cleveland and Jared R. Price, "The Failure of Federal Aviation Administration Regulation, *The Independent Review*, Summer 2003.

Chapter 5: Agricultural Policy

Farming has long been viewed nostalgically by Americans. There may be many reasons for this. For instance, it might be because early on in our nation's history most Americans were involved in agricultural pursuits. Certainly, these endeavors were the backbone of the economy in those days. In fact, the desire to own and farm one's own piece of land provided many immigrants ample incentive to come to the United States in the first place. Regrettably, this nostalgia also led to the acceptance of policies aimed at providing farmers with a privileged position in society. The results of such privilege have led to the development of an overbearing bureaucracy; known today as the United States Department of Agriculture; that controls agricultural pursuits. The thrust of its policies today tends to raise farm product prices while it funnels taxpayers' money to certain business interests. The process by which this behemoth arose began during the Civil War.

In discussing matters of history, it is easy to forget that life goes on even during war. That was true of the activities of Congress while presiding over government during the Civil War. That Congress passed numerous pieces of legislation that had little to do with the war effort, but had major ramifications for the direction that public policy would take for many years to come. Actually, the war made it easier for the passage of some of the legislation. As mentioned in earlier chapters, there had always been a contingent that was interested in adopting mercantilistic policies. Alexander Hamilton, Henry Clay, the Whig party, and the new Republican party, all favored policies whereby government force would be used for the purpose of promoting various business interests. Until the war, those interests had been largely held in check first by the Jeffersonian Republicans and then by the Jacksonian Democrats. Since the democrats were largely of Southern origin, the secession of the South from the union resulted in the absence of many congressmen and senators who would have opposed some of the legislation that was put into law during this time. Their absence essentially provided the republicans a free hand to enact all sorts of new policies based upon their mercantilistic ideals.

The Morrill Tariff Act of 1861, the Morrill Land Grant Act of 1862, the Homestead Act of 1862, and the Pacific Railway Act were among the key pieces of legislation that extended the presence of the government's hand into business affairs in the nation.[60] The Morrill Tariff Act significantly raised tariffs in an effort to protect Northern manufacturing interests. It was increased in 1864 and thus became even more protectionistic. This further raised the prices of many products. Among those products affected by the policy were many capital goods used by farmers. This legislation diminished the profit margins generally maintained by the nation's farmers.

As we have already seen, the Pacific Railway Act, coupled with the Homestead Act, led to the rapid expansion of the west far faster than would have been the case apart from the government's support and subsidy. This led to new lands coming into farm production earlier than they would have otherwise. New farmers meant an increase in output which drove agricultural product prices down and put even more pressure on marginal and sub-marginal farmers in both the west and the east.

In addition to the impact of these pieces of legislation, the Morrill Land Grant Act made large tracts of land available to the states for the purpose of founding agricultural and technical colleges. The thinking behind this policy was that these institutions would be involved in research that would enhance the productivity of farmers. On the surface such a policy would appear to be of great benefit to the farmers except for the unintended consequences necessarily associated with it. While it is true that these institutions did make available new techniques

---

[60] Two excellent references in the discussion of agriculture include Clarence Carson, *The War on the Poor*, (Phenix City, AL: American Textbook Committee, 1969) and Clarence Carson, *A Basic History of the United States: The Sections and the Civil War 1826-1877*, (Phenix City, AL: American Textbook Committee, 1985).

that improved the productivity of farmers, it is also true that this enhanced the problems already being faced by the marginal and sub-marginal farmers of that day. The reason that this is so is because greater productivity by farmers results in lower agricultural product prices. When combined with the other policies instituted, many people involved in agricultural pursuits found themselves caught under an economic rock. They simply were not able to make their financial ends meet and found their costs rising as their revenues declined.

In an effort to hang onto their businesses many looked to blame others and sought relief by seeking additional government action. We have already seen how and why the farmers tried to blame the railroads for their plight. The government responded by imposing new regulations on railroads, by extending tariff coverage to agricultural products, and by offering farmers easy credit. But these policies could hardly help. First, the regulations essentially meant that transportation would be operated as a government run cartel. That would not and did not result in lower transportation costs. The extension of tariffs to include more agricultural products was ineffective as well because the United States was a net exporter of such products. Thus, protectionist tariffs made little difference to the economic situation. If the tariffs had any impact at all, the overall effect of them was to reduce the amount of export opportunities of America's farmers as other nations responded in kind to the U.S. policy. An increase in foreign tariffs on U.S products simply makes them more expensive and thus reduces the size of the foreign market. Once again this worked to the disadvantage of the farmer.

Finally, easy credit is not a solution for people involved in a failing business enterprise. The fact that lenders are unwilling to lend someone money at a low rate merely reflects something about the business risk involved in the undertaking. If the government intervenes to cut this rate artificially it keeps some people in a business activity far longer than they would have stayed otherwise. As a result, the final business failure is even harder to bear. Nevertheless, the government began moving to promote easy credit for farmers during this time.

From this point in time throughout the end of the nineteenth century and up until the 1930s, the government continued to pursue combinations of these policies. Thus, legislators and bureaucrats created a series of booms and busts in farming as situations in the agricultural industry fluctuated. This was especially true of the 1920s. The early twenties were largely problematic for American farmers as the revival of agricultural production in Europe reduced the size of the markets they had enjoyed immediately following World War I. The war had devastated Europe and it took some time to restore the capital that had been lost because of it. As a result, American farmers benefited greatly from an increase in the demand for their goods. However, by the twenties this situation was reversing itself. In an effort to aid the farmers whose market size was dwindling, the government pursued easy credit policies that expanded the nation's money supply.[61] The easy money policy pursued during the twenties led to a rapid economic boom which later gave way to a bust as we saw in the earlier chapter on monetary policy.

In addition to the easy money policy, the agricultural industry underwent some major structural changes that were brought about by technological advancements that were adopted. Among these was the development of new farm equipment that employed internal combustion engines. Replacing horse drawn plows with tractors greatly extended the productivity of the individual farmer. The adoption of this new technology meant that each individual farmer was able to produce a much larger output and this put downward pressure on farm product prices. This process, which economist Joseph Schumpeter referred to creative destruction, is part of the market process. The market is not static, but follows a dynamic process of change and that

---

[61] For an excellent discourse on the boom of the 1920s which led to the depression of the 1930s see, Murray N. Rothbard, *America's Great Depression*, (Princeton, NJ: D. Van Nostrand Company, 1963).

means that the fortunes of individual people may ebb and flow as entrepreneurial successes take place. In general, though some fortunes may wane, such advancements nonetheless improve the common welfare as fewer resources are devoted to the production of specific goods. As a result, prices generally fall and people find that they are able to afford a greater variety of goods and services than they were able to beforehand.

Unfortunately, the combination of the government's easy credit policy, coupled with the presence of rapid technological change, meant that the process of creative destruction was sped up so to speak. That is, more farmers purchased more of the new equipment than was warranted by the economic facts. In addition, more companies entered into the production of such equipment than would prove profitable in the long run. Moreover, this problem was compounded by the many firms that developed to supply the resources for the larger manufacturing interests. In essence, the combination of the facts of the case led to numerous mal-investments in capital. Many of these investments would eventually fail to be profitable and when this was realized a collapse would come. The collapse of certain markets began in 1929 when it became increasingly obvious to many people that their capital investments were not economically sound.

In such situations, the best policy the government might adopt to deal with the resulting recession is to leave the economy alone. However, that has not been what most government officials have chosen to do in such situations. Rather, they typically pursue actions that tend to exacerbate the recession. Among the policies officials typically pursue on such occasions are attempts to prevent the liquidation of unsound businesses by lending additional funds to them, attempts to re-inflate the money supply, attempts to keep prices high in general and wages up in particular, attempts to encourage consumption and to penalize saving, and attempts to provide subsidies for

unemployment.[62] Each of these actions keeps some people
hanging on to certain business ventures that are simply not
economic and at the same time lead to confusion among other
market participants because numerous prices are masked and
distorted. As a result, the process of economic reallocation of
assets is hindered and the recession is lengthened. This is what
happened in the 1930s as a result of the policies of both the
Hoover and Roosevelt administrations. The Roosevelt
administration was especially adept in preventing the recovery
and set in place new agricultural policies that have plagued the
industry to this day.

When Franklin Roosevelt came into the office of the
presidency in 1933, he proposed to offer the people a New Deal,
as he called it. As one historian put the matter, there were four
fundamental motivations behind the sweeping policy proposals
that were summed up as being part of the New Deal. These
include a commitment Roosevelt and his administration had to
inflationary monetary policy, their commitment to progressivism,
their desire to mobilize government action as it had been during
World War I, and their desire to implement national economic
planning in an effort to move the U.S. toward socialism by
adopting fascism as the nation's basic form of political-economic
system.[63] Among the efforts of the administration to pursue their
collectivist policies was the Agricultural Adjustment Act which
was passed in 1933. The new agency of the government created
by this act immediately set out to develop and implement policies
aimed at increasing farm product prices. The bureaucrats took
their job so seriously that they actually paid cotton farmers to
plow up standing fields of cotton and bought up some six million
small pigs to kill them in order to keep them off the market.[64]
While this was the only time that such measures were
undertaken, the fact that the government actually intervened to

---

[62] Ibid, pg. 26.
[63] Clarence Carson, *A Basic History of the United States: The Welfare State 1929-1985*, (Phenix City, AL:
American Textbook Committee, 1986), pp. 34-37.
[64] Ibid., pp. 52-54.

destroy produce does give us some good understanding of the fundamental problem associated with the whole effort.

Suppose you were a cast away, alone on a deserted island, and that there were limited means for your survival. Suppose further that there were only two coconut trees on the island and these served to provide you with some basic sustenance. To be sure your economic circumstances would be somewhat dire. However, it would not be to your benefit to cut down and burn one of the coconut trees in an attempt to raise the price of coconuts. That would be the dumbest thing that you could do. The action would certainly make coconuts more costly, but that fact would be to your own economic detriment and not to your economic well being. Despite this economic truth, the meddling spirit of the government planners of the 1930s insured that the people of the United States would be made to live through harder times than those they were already enduring by imposing policies that made the situation worse.

In years following this initial activity, the agricultural bureaucracy moved to implement numerous policies that were aimed at cutting production of farm products and raising farm product prices. Among these included limitations in the amounts of acreage that might be allotted to grow certain crops, the establishment of price floors to insure that the legal price could not fall below some government prescribed level, and, of course, easy credit that would allow farmers to finance holding some of their produce off of the market. In essence, the government had created an elaborate labyrinth of rules and regulations that prevented private individuals from engaging in agricultural pursuits on terms that they found agreeable to them. Instead, one must succumb to government restrictions and red tape if he wishes to engage in such an enterprise.

These rules and regulations have resulted in more than a little twisting and turning of logic in the years since they were first imposed. In fact, every few years since the New Deal, Congress has passed legislation that updates the nation's official farm policies. When rightly understood, some of the policies simply boggle the mind. However, because of the costs associated with actually understanding what the government is up to, most people have no idea about the details of the farm bills that have been passed. To get some understanding of the effects of government regulation it will be worthwhile to consider a couple of areas of government involvement. Toward that end, it will be worthwhile to examine the price floors imposed on the production and sale of milk and the maintenance of price floors on the production of sugar which also include limits on production and strict quotas on importation.

The imposition of policies aimed at controlling dairy prices date back to the New Deal. Since then an elaborate system of controls has been instituted and is continually updated. Among the policies most prominent in the dairy industry is the imposition of price floors. As any student of economics should clearly understand, effective price floors invariably create surpluses. When governments intervene in markets and mandate legal prices above those that would prevail in a free market the effect is that producers will offer more for sale than the buying public wishes to purchase. As a result, a surplus of the product occurs. Indeed, that is what has happened in the dairy industry. Under the terms of the policy, the government buys and stores the dairy surpluses at taxpayers' expense. As one researcher observed:

> In the early years of the dairy supports and into the 1970s, the direct cost of the program to taxpayers ranged annually from $69 million to $612 million, with an average of $325 million. The 1970s brought higher inflation and strong pressure from dairy lobbyists to increase milk price supports... By the 1980s, high price supports resulted in the CCC's [(the Commodity Credit Corporation of the USDA)] spending $1 billion per year to support dairy prices. In 1983 the CCC spent a record $2.6 billion to

purchase 16.8 billion pounds of milk products—more than 12 percent of the total U.S. milk production.[65]

As is clear from this research, the federal government had to buy up large quantities of surplus dairy products in the 1980s. As the cost of this program continued to escalate, the government began to look for other options. In November 1983, the government launched a program aimed at reducing the amount of dairy production by buying dairy cattle from farmers. "At the end of the first dairy supply reduction program in early 1985, after $995 million had been spent, there were only 10,000 fewer dairy cows in the United States than there had been at the beginning. The USDA paid the equivalent of $100,000 for each net cow reduction of the total American dairy herd, even though a used dairy cow is worth less than $1,000."[66] Despite the utter failure of this first program, Congress tried the same approach again in 1986-1987. The federal government paid out over $1.3 billion for dairy cows and had them put on the market for slaughter. However, once again the program had no perceivable impact on dairy production.[67]

The entire program continues to be costly for U.S. taxpayers who have been forced to shoulder the burden of providing benefits to privileged dairy farmers. According to GAO estimates, the cost of government's milk price support program is expected to run about $2.0 billion annually for fiscal years 2002 until 2007. Of that annual amount, $1.6 billion is expected to be spent each year purchasing surplus dairy products.[68] In effect, this one federal program is expected to cost an average family of four more than $160 over this six year period of time and that amount does not include the extra money each family will have

---

[65] Kevin McNew, "Milking the Sacred Cow: A Case for Eliminating the Federal Dairy Program," *Policy Analysis No. 362*, The Cato Institute, December 1999, pp. 6-7.

[66] James Bovard, "Our Next Criminal Class: Milk Bootleggers," *Cato Briefing Paper No. 13*, June 1991, pg. 4.

[67] Ibid., pg. 4.

[68] "Department of Agriculture, Commodity Credit Corporation: 2002 Farm Bill Regulations," GAO-03-245R, February 26, 2004.

to pay for dairy products simply because the government has chosen to keep these product prices above what they would have been in a free market.

As expensive as the milk program is, the sugar program is even more twisted. When one begins investigating this program, one finds a perverse program aimed at providing a handful of people with huge economic profits while imposing costs on virtually all other Americans. As is the case for many of the current federal programs, the fundamental direction of the modern sugar program can be dated back to the Roosevelt administration, though the history of intervention is even longer. Nonetheless, acreage allotments, price supports, and cheap loan options for sugar cane and beet farmers became a fundamental part of the industry in the 1930s.

One of the main differences between the sugar program and the milk program is that the government aimed not to have to deal with the surplus that the price floor invariably creates. Toward that end, the government imposed strict rules on the amount of acreage that could be devoted to sugar production and maintained strict quotas on the amount of sugar that could be imported. In this way, the government has for the most part been able to avoid dealing with a sugar surplus; however, it has had to purchase large amounts of the product from producers in recent years.[69] The presence of an actual surplus notwithstanding, as the principles of economics suggest, the impact of the government's program has been to keep U.S. sugar prices higher than they would have been otherwise. "Congressmen justify the sugar program as protecting Americans from the 'roller-coaster of international sugar prices,' as Congressman Byron Dorgan declared. Unfortunately, Congress protects consumers against the 'roller-coaster' by pegging American sugar prices on the level of the Goodyear blimp, floating far above the amusement park."[70]

---

[69] James Bovard, "Sink the Sugar Boondoggle," *The Future of Freedom Foundation*, September 2001.
[70] Jame Bovard, *The Farm Fiasco*, (San Francisco, CA: ICS Press, 1989), pg. 62.

One of the more interesting details of the sugar program is the corporate rent seeking that has been spawned by the program's existence. Indeed, since the establishment of the current program, a sugar lobby has developed that wishes to maintain it because of the immense benefits received. In the 1970s that sugar lobby added another crucial participant to its group. That participant was and is a large agribusiness firm known as ADM (Archer Daniels Midland).[71] ADM had gotten into the production and sale of a product known as high fructose corn syrup. Their motivation for entering the business was the fact that sugar prices were at an all time high and the production of a competitive product made sense. That was until the bottom fell out of the sugar market and prices dropped quickly. Undeterred by this problem, ADM's managers pushed ahead with their product and sought to secure its market by lobbying to keep sugar prices in America high. As a result, the company has become one of the chief financiers of the political lobby. In the presidential election of 1992, sources indicate that between the company and its CEO almost $1.4 million was donated to the candidates. That is, donations were made to both parties and both candidates.[72] Of course, ADM is not alone in this effort. From 1979 to 1995, "sugar-related interests (sugar cane, beet, and corn sweeteners) have invested more than $11.9 million in the campaigns of candidates for federal office and political parties."[73] In an effort to insure the passage of the most recent farm bill in 2002, some $4.3 million was donated to federal political candidates by those in the sugar industry. Clearly, the benefits for those on the inside of this industry are huge. The aim of these political expenditures is evident. The business interests involved wish to maintain their privileged position in America by seeing to it that members of Congress continue the

---

[71] For an excellent discussion of ADM and its practices in rent seeking see, James Bovard, "Archer Daniels Midland: A Case Study in Corporate Welfare," *Cato Policy Analysis No. 241*, September 1995.

[72] Ibid., pg. 3.

[73] Ellen S. Miller, "The Politics of Sugar," *Center for Responsive Politics*, May 1995.

sugar program well into the future. The GAO has estimated that the total cost of the program was about $1.5 billion in 1996 and about $1.9 billion in 1998.[74]

In these two programs, one is able to see how political meddling has led to continued intrigue as some individuals use the nation's laws to direct taxpayers' dollars into their pockets. In addition, they reveal how such government rules drive up prices beyond what would have prevailed otherwise. As a result, Americans generally are worse off today because of the existence of the Department of Agriculture and the cumbersome rules and regulations that prevent farm product markets from functioning well. It has been estimated that the latest farm bill will cost the average family almost $4,400 in taxes and higher food prices over the ten year period from 2002 to 2012.[75]

Regrettably, the likelihood that such programs will actually be ended is slim. The average American is simply unaware of what is really going on with these pieces of legislation. In contrast, the immediate material gains for both politicians and lobbying interests are high. Therefore, the Congress is most likely to continue to behave as they have in the past and will most likely continue to promote such programs.

---

[74] "Sugar Program: Supporting Sugar Prices has Increased Users' Costs While Benefiting Producers," GAO/RCED-93-84, June 2000.
[75] Brian M. Riedl, "Agriculture Lobby Wins Big in the New Farm Bill," *The Heritage Foundation Backgrounder No. 1534*, April 9, 2002.

Chapter 6: Education Policy

Education is an important factor in providing the underlying support for a growing and vibrant economy. While the pursuit of academic interests may be postponed, once a community is reasonably well-fed, clothed, and housed, the people who populate it invariably turn their attention to intellectual interests. Indeed, men naturally desire to work smarter and not harder in order to achieve their ends and it is the human capacity to think, plan, and act that best allows for human flourishing. In addition, human beings are creatures of the mind so to speak. They express the spiritual essence of themselves in their artistic endeavors and these efforts are as much a matter of promoting human well-being as is obtaining the needed material wherewithal to provide for one's subsistence. As a result, people have always understood the value of training their minds in order to engage the world in which they live with greater clarity and effectiveness. Nevertheless, such pursuits are inevitably subordinated to the essential material needs of survival.

Historically speaking, communities were formed around agrarian pursuits. The more successful these pursuits were, the more the community could develop in complex ways. It was based upon such success that academic enterprises flourished. As a result, people in such successful communities could begin to take advantage of their varying talents. In truth, the material well-being of the people in a community allowed them the opportunity to devote more interest to the arts and sciences and the things of the human mind and spirit. This is the natural progression of things.

In America, the interest in education was intensified on religious grounds. The large bulk of the early settlers were refugees from the religious wars that were taking place in Europe in association with the Protestant Reformation. The settlers were mainly Protestant in their religious views. This was a significant fact because one of the key issues of the Reformation had been the debate over what constituted the primary authority in doctrinal matters. Those advocating the Roman Catholic position argued that sound Christian doctrine was founded upon the combination of the Scriptures coupled with Church traditions. Alternatively, those people of a Protestant mindset argued that Christian doctrines were founded on Scripture alone as exhibited in their rallying cry *Sola Scriptura*. They rejected the formal Roman Catholic Church for its failure to teach and promote the Christian religion as it is taught in the Scriptures. Instead, they believed that it was every person's responsibility to read and adhere to the teachings of the Bible. As Susan Alder has put it:

> The privilege of communion with and intimate access to God, which came through the reading of the Word and prayer, no longer remained the right of a priestly hierarchy but was open to all who believed. The responsibility of knowing God and thinking his thoughts after him required a thorough knowledge of his Holy Word, the Bible. This mandated that believers be literate; it also mandated that education be part of evangelism.[76]

The reason that this is important in understanding the development of America's education system is that this view carries with it the belief that each man is responsible for reading God's Word and for living his life in accordance with it. People who believe that this is true, must also believe that it is important that people learn to read in order to be able to study the Bible. That motivation provided the early Americans with all the incentive needed to establish and develop numerous schools and other institutions of learning.

These institutions were largely church related and were,

---

[76] Susan Alder, "Education in America", *The Freeman*, (Irvington, NY: Foundation for Economic Education, February 1993), pg. 59.

thus, private. While some local authorities got involved in education, there was no systematic effort on the part of the federal, state, or local governments to control it. For example, the Massachusetts Bay Colony maintained compulsory education laws early on and founded and ran schools. However, this effort did not undercut private educators who eventually put the local authorities out of the education business. In this case, the involvement amounted to an effort to insure that people were taught to read and this was done primarily for religious reasons. In a very real sense, the Massachusetts laws followed the traditional form of local law in European communities which tended to mix the affairs of the church with political rule. But the involvement of the government in the Massachusetts example was not the norm. Generally speaking, the entire education system in early America was one that was privately established, run, and maintained.

In a very real sense, education in colonial America was Christian. Church schools sprang up throughout the colonies with the intention of evangelizing the community. Perhaps the greatest work of these efforts is seen in the Great Awakening. Preachers like George Whitefield traversed the countryside bringing the good news to people. His success resulted in many new converts who needed education. As a result, many new schools and colleges were started. Most of the schools and educational opportunities were, therefore, sponsored by churches to meet the needs of local congregations or as a basis of extending charity to others in the community. Teaching materials were thoroughly Christian as well, which is evident if one looks at the contents of Noah Webster's dictionary or William Holmes McGuffey's reader.

It was not until the very late eighteenth century that there was any real interest in establishing state education. Even then, it was viewed as an educational opportunity of last resort. There wasn't any compulsion to send one's children to any of the state schools which were set up with limited use of tax dollars for support. Most people ignored such schools altogether. However, the Unitarians of the time continued to push for government control to get poorer people out of Christian mission schools. By the middle of the nineteenth century these people were beginning to have influence upon local and state governments and the number of state schools was growing. Their efforts were aided by three factors including the spread of a social gospel, the influx of a large number of Catholic immigrants, and the compromise of religious principle.

   Among the most ardent of the Unitarian voices of the time was Horace Mann who is often considered to be the father of the public schools.[77] The term itself being misleading since what Mann advocated was a common, government run school for all. What Mann sought was the forced taxation of people to support government run institutions in which young children would be socialized. In essence, Mann's aim was to undercut whatever doctrinal distinctives that a child's parents might favor in order to promote a common set of values. By doing so, Mann thought divisions among people would fade away and society would be transformed into a common pool of likeminded people. In this regard, Mann was a socialist utopian of sorts and most assuredly a reformist in his thinking. He feared private schools as a constant threat to his concept of the common school and was especially opposed to private Christian education. He rationalized the forced imposition of taxes to pay for such schools as a necessary price to guarantee freedom. In this view, one is reminded of Rousseau's comment in his *Social Contract* that men might need to be forced to be free. Of course such statements are just so much nonsense and certainly Mann's concept of freedom was abysmally lacking at this point. Nevertheless, that is what he thought and that is what he pushed for. He made quite a bit of headway toward his goals in his home state of Massachusetts where he served for some time on the state's Board of Education.

---

[77] For a brief biography of Horace Mann see, Horace Mann, *The Republic and the School*, edited by Lawrence Cremin (Bureau of Publications Teachers College, Columbia University, 1957), pp. 3-28.

While the efforts of people like Mann might have come to nothing, they were aided by the times. There was a large influx of Catholic immigrants coming to America from the early to middle and latter part of the nineteenth century and the Protestant majority of the time viewed this negatively. Since the Sunday school movement in churches was well under way, many Christians began to embrace the rapid expansion of state education as a means of preserving "Protestant Christian America." "But in looking to the state schools, Christians made two costly mistakes: They turned from persuasion to coercion, from evangelism to state education for the preservation of their society. They also abandoned their own parental responsibility."[78] As a result, government schools began to spread and were further promoted by the adoption of compulsory attendance laws. This provided an education system that might be used for the purpose of instilling upon young minds one form of propaganda or another.

One of the main problems of this kind of thinking is that it assumes that someone is able to discern and impose the best kind of propaganda. It assumes that the best way to provide a robust education is known to some and is only in need of being disseminated by employing the collective force of government. However, this notion is at best just pure vanity. Nobel Prize winning economist, Friedrich Hayek, spent much of his career refuting the misguided notions of social engineers. In his book, *The Fatal Conceit: The Errors of Socialism*, [79] Hayek destroyed any scientific position which might be claimed by those seeking to recreate human nature and human institutions for utopian purposes. In destroying the socialist argument he wrote:

> So, priding itself on having built its world as if it had designed it, and blaming itself for not having designed it better, humankind is now to set out to

---

[78] Susan Adler, op. cit., pg. 64.
[79] Friedrich A. Hayek, *The Fatal Conceit: The Errors of Socialism*, ed. by W.W. Bartley III, The University of Chicago Press: Chicago, 1988.

do just that. The aim of socialism is no less than to effect a complete redesigning of our traditional morals, law, and language, and on this basis to stamp out the old order and the supposedly inexorable, unjustifiable conditions that prevent the institution of reason, fulfillment, true freedom, and justice.[80]

Hayek understood rightly that knowledge of any subject is something that grows over the course of time as a result of continuous study and discovery. Since human knowledge of anything is always truncated, there is always room for improvement and that progress is most likely to be made in an environment that is unfettered by governmental busybodies whose aim is to foist their ideas upon others. This is as true for the process of education as it is of any other human enterprise. In essence, Horace Mann and his kind engaged actively in the "fatal conceit" of assuming that they alone knew more than anyone else. While someone might well have better ideas about how to provide educational opportunities for others, only a free market can provide a satisfactory test of that assertion.

In this vein, another writer, French economist, Frederic Bastiat, addressed the same issues of socialism in his own country in 1850. Like Hayek, he too clearly characterized the fatal conceit of socialism as a solution to any of our problems.

Present-day writers—especially those of the socialist school of thought—base their various theories upon one common hypothesis: They divide mankind into two parts. People in general—with the exception of the writer himself—form the first group. The writer, all alone, forms the second and most important group. Surely this is the weirdest and most conceited notion that ever entered a human brain!

In fact, these writers on public affairs begin by

---

[80] Ibid, p.67.

supposing that people have within themselves no means of discernment; no motivation to action. The writers assume that people are inert matter, passive particles, motionless atoms, at best a kind of vegetation indifferent to its own manner of existence. They assume that people are susceptible to being shaped—by the will and hand of another person—into an infinite variety of forms, more or less symmetrical, artistic, and perfected. Moreover, not one of these writers on governmental affairs hesitates to imagine himself—under the title of organizer, discoverer, legislator, or founder—is this will and hand, this universal motivating force, this creative power whose sublime mission is to mold these scattered materials—persons—into a society...

Socialists look upon people as raw material to be formed into social combinations...Moreover, even where they have consented to recognize a principle of action in the heart of man—and a principle of discernment in man's intellect—they have considered these gifts from God to be fatal gifts. They have thought that persons, under the impulse of these two gifts, would fatally tend to ruin themselves. They assume that if the legislators left persons free to follow their own inclinations, they would arrive at atheism instead of religion, ignorance instead of knowledge, poverty instead of production and exchange.[81]

What Bastiat understood well was that children are not a kind of vegetation or a mass of cells in need of being molded into the image of some educational or political potter. Rather, they are real human beings who need to be nurtured in a way

---

[81] Frederic Bastiat, *The Law*, The Foundation for Economic Education: Irvington-on-Hudson, New York, 1987, pp 33-36.

that allows them to best exploit their own innate talents and abilities in a reasonable and systematic way. Nevertheless, the reformist and socialist ideas of education that were being promoted in the process of adopting and spreading government schools had at its heart an antihuman concept of children. This fact opened the door for other reformists whose efforts began to further divert America's education system from an institution for the training of young minds so that they could excel for themselves into a political indoctrination center aimed at stripping young people of their humanity in order to make them fit for operating in a statist complex.

One such reformer was John Dewey. Dewey is well-known for his promotion of the philosophy of pragmatism and for his ideas about how this philosophy should shape the educational process. Dewey thought that knowledge was merely a social construct. He rejected any notion that there were any absolute truths. Instead, he embraced the relativistic thought of his age that flowed from a commitment to ideological naturalism that was spawned by the Enlightenment. Like Mann, Dewey embraced the common school movement as a means of socializing people into a common pool. He focused his educational philosophy on the notion that the system ought to be child centered. This philosophy immediately placed Dewey at odds with those who maintained religious conceptions of the nature of this universe in which we live. In their view, we can know something because God already knows everything that there is to know. Since we are his creatures and have been created with the capacity to know, real knowledge is possible by way of discovery. This difference in conception of the nature of truth has resulted in an ongoing culture war between competing interests for control over the school system and its curriculum of choice. For the most part, the naturalist perspective has tended to become the one that has been enshrined in nation's educational system much to the chagrin of those who embrace a religious worldview. While many of those on the losing side of this trend bemoan people like Dewey, the truth is that the entire system was originally spawned within the conceptions of a socialistic worldview. In fact, the religiously minded people should have known better than to embrace the common school movement in the first place since its relativism is fundamental to its purpose and men like Dewey were merely expressing the natural progression of their own beliefs.

Whatever lasting impact Dewey has had on America's educational system and its curriculum, one thing can be said with certainty about the common school movement. Namely, it is thought of as a place where individuality is displaced by a pervasive sameness in the hopes of promoting corporate unity among the people of the community. Put simply, it is a collectivist notion that regards the individual person as having no value apart from the collective. In practice, the fundamental purpose of the common school and the egalitarian principles upon which it is founded tend to result in a steady pressure for greater central control over the system. Those who accept the purpose of socializing human beings into the American collective will readily push for this kind of centralized control. In effect, they will work to ensure a tighter government monopoly over the entire system starting with local government control, then pressing to control at the state level, and finally pressing for federal control over the educational system. Indeed, that has been the direction that educational reform has taken.

The progression of centralizing control moved steadily from the local level, to the increasing involvement of state politicians and bureaucrats, and finally to the involvement of federal authorities. Joel Spring provided an excellent review of this progression in his book *American Education*.[82] Local control over schools began to be eroded by state action in the latter part of the nineteenth century with the passage of compulsory attendance laws by state legislatures. These acts immediately brought state authorities into some level of control over

---

[82] Joel Spring, *American Education: An Introduction to the Social and Political Aspects*, (New York: Longman, 4th edition, 1989). In particular see chapters 6-8.

education since they required some effort to insure their enforcement. As a result, a new level of administration was imposed which varied from state to state depending upon the guidelines drafted to define what might constitute an acceptable level of school attendance. Some states went so far as to attempt to require all parents to send their children to state funded government schools. However, this attempt was met with sharp resistance and was eventually ruled to be a violation of the parents' constitutional rights. Nevertheless, in each state, there developed a set of bureaucratic rules and regulations that govern the definition of what constitutes an acceptable school for compliance purposes. These rules have extended so far as to promote curriculum requirements that must be met if the school is to comply with state mandates. In essence, each state government assumes for itself the right to impose upon the families within its jurisdiction its own definition of what constitutes a suitable education. The result of this effort is that education has become increasingly politicized.

The process of politicization has intensified over the years as the issue of education itself has become increasingly important during elections. As a result, politicians typically pander to certain interest groups in an effort to secure the needed votes to get themselves elected. Such pandering typically undercuts the quality of whatever education is actually delivered by the government schools since the proposals and resulting programs of these politicians are typically costly and impose new compliance requirements on the schools. As a result, the natural progression is that more funds are expended on administrative issues while less are devoted to actual classroom instruction.

The federal government's involvement in education began to pick up speed in the late 1950s with the passage of the National Defense Education Act of 1958. Under the guise of promoting national defense, this act provided federal authorities an indirect means of controlling the nation's education system thus further centralizing control. The act operated by offering local school districts federal funds if they would adopt certain programs, materials, and curricula. In this way, federal authorities began to use taxpayers' funds to bribe local school officials. Once the federal coffers were opened, the offer of such funds tended to be readily pursued and this set in motion the process of greater and greater federal involvement in education as additional laws were passed and as more rules and regulations governing the use of federal funds were established.

For example, during the 1960s the Johnson administration expanded the Elementary and Secondary Education Act of 1965. This legislation was part of Johnson's Great Society programs aimed at addressing poverty in the United States. In essence, this legislation took at face value the idea that the lack of education is one of the key factors in explaining poverty and that it could be alleviated by funneling federal money to fund the educations of poorer students. Thus, the act made funds available for the purpose of establishing programs aimed at this segment of society. It was in this way, that many people came to believe that one could not achieve upward mobility economically speaking apart from attaining a particular kind of education. While the two appear to be positively correlated, that exact relationship seems far from certain especially when it is realized that the richest man in America did not finish his college degree. The truth is knowledge about anything in particular is much broader than completing a set of degree requirements and that it is often possible in a market economy to put knowledge obtained apart from formal schooling to one's economic advantage.

Beyond using carrots as a means of controlling education, the federal government has also used another device, the stick as it were, in its effort to extend its control. Namely, now that the schools have become more dependent on federal funding, the government threatens local school districts with the reduction in existing funding if it fails to comply with additional laws it passes. This extortionist approach to achieving compliance began to be used in earnest during the 1960s in conjunction with the Civil Rights laws which were passed during that period. The government adopted the policy that any school that failed to abide by the discrimination guidelines drawn up by federal authorities would lose any federal funding it had already been receiving. Beyond these kinds of mandates, the federal courts of the country also began to intervene in the educational system by reaching decisions that imposed various additional mandates on local communities. In this way the federal bureaucracy of control escalated.

What happened as a result of this approach is that school districts were forced to expend more and more of their available resources to insure compliance with federal mandates. In time, the rules, regulations, and guidelines expanded and became more and more cumbersome and costly. They diverted scarce resources from the classroom to administrative issues and thus undercut the quality of education that was actually delivered. Furthermore, just as education was politicized at the state level, so too was it politicized at the national level. One attempt to streamline federal control came in the 1980s during the Reagan administration. Reagan sought to reduce the red tape imposed on local schools by offering them block grants and providing them with much broader ability to choose how federal funding could be spent. However, this approach invited the criticism that it allowed school districts too much latitude in spending federal funds and there were new calls for greater oversight. To be sure, that is the context in which federal funding of education operates today. The controls imposed on local school districts tend to be driven by the attitudes of the current administration whoever they may be. Some prefer greater oversight and impose longer lists of requirements for federal compliance and others opt for shorter lists. Nevertheless, federal oversight and bureaucratic wrangling is well established.

The costs associated with education tell the story. In the academic year 1969-1970 there was an average daily attendance of students in public schools of 41,934,376 students. In the academic year 1999-2000 that figure was 43,806,726.[83] That represents a difference of just under 2,000,000 students or about a four and one half percent increase. Despite the rather flat level of student attendance in public schools, real spending in constant 2001-2002 dollars increased from $192 billion to $402 billion which represents a 109 percent increase in spending.[84] Despite spending such large additional sums of money, there has been no improvement in the quality of the education as evidenced by student test scores. In truth, what has grown has been the level of bureaucratic red tape, and the associated increase in administrative expenditures. In the most recent years, the federal government has passed a new piece of legislation known as the No Child Left Behind Act which is almost certain to expand federal government's authority and bureaucracy even further. This act reauthorized the earlier provisions of the ESEA legislation and extended it with provisions calling for expanded accountability to federally mandated goals. As such, it will further hinder local schools from actually delivering a better education to their students as they expend ever greater amounts of resources attempting to comply with the new mandates so that they will not lose their current federal funding.

One of the fundamental problems associated with a government educational monopoly is that it presumes itself capable of identifying and implementing the best and most perfect system. However, such a presumption is pure vanity at best. In fact, we live in a world where our knowledge of it is very imperfect. We simply do not know what might be the "best" way of doing anything in general and certainly not of providing the "best" possible schooling in particular. Nevertheless, establishing and running a governmental education monopoly presupposes that the bureaucrats that run it are infallible. We would do well to consider the words of the nineteenth century economists,

---

[83] U.S. Department of Education, National Center for Education Statistics, *Revenues and Expenditures for Public and Secondary Education*, Table 41, May 2002.
[84] Ibid., Table 30.

Frederic Bastiat who wrote:

> ...if people could agree on the best possible kind of
> education, in regard to both the content and
> method, a uniform system of public instruction
> would be preferable, since error would, in that case,
> be necessarily excluded by law. But as long as such a
> criterion has not been found, as long as the legislator
> and the Minister of Public Education do not carry
> on their persons an unquestionable sign of
> infallibility, the true method has the best chance of
> being discovered and of displacing the others if room
> is left for diversity, trial by error, experimentation,
> and individual efforts guided by a self-regarding
> interest in the outcome—in a word, where there is
> freedom. The chances are worst in a uniform system
> of education established by decree, for in such a
> system error is permanent, universal, and
> irremediable. Therefore, those who, in the name of
> fraternity, demand that the law determine what shall
> be taught and impose this on everyone should realize
> that they are running the risk of having the law
> direct and impose teaching of nothing but error; for
> legal interdiction can pervert the truth by perverting
> the minds that believe they have possession of it.
> Now is it, I ask, fraternity, in the true sense of the
> word, that has recourse to force to impose, or at least
> to run the risk of imposing, error on mankind?
> Diversity is feared: it is stigmatized as anarchy. But it
> results necessarily from the very diversity of men's
> opinions and convictions, a diversity that tends,
> besides, to disappear with discussion, study, and
> experience. In the meanwhile, what claim has one
> system to prevail over any other by law or force? Here
> again we find that this pretended fraternity, which

invokes the law or legal constraint, is in opposition to justice.[85]

In this quote, Bastiat captured well the central problem with governmental monopolies of any kind. The directors of them must assume that they know more than anyone else. In fact, they must assume that they know everything that there is to know regarding the subject at hand. However, that knowledge is never actually present with them. In fact, they do not know more and in many cases they know less. Economic progress, material well-being, and quality improvements in goods and services comes about in an environment where people are free to trade on terms that they find mutually agreeable with the seller of the good. In such circumstances, providers of services are compelled to deliver the products that the consumers are willing to pay for. The competitive pressures of this process invariably lead to improvements over time. Regrettably, this process has been short circuited in education.

---

[85] Frederic Bastiat, *Selected Essays on Political Economy*, (Irvington-on-Hudson, NY: The Foundation for Economic Education, 1995), pp. 131-132.

Chapter 7: Labor Policy

The Grant of Political Power to Labor Unions in the 1930's

Prior to the New Deal years of Franklin Roosevelt, the nation had no particular significant policies regarding labor. For the most part employers and employees were free to contract on mutually agreeable terms. Within this context, employees sometimes formed unions as a means of collectively bargaining with employers in the hopes of securing a better deal. Such voluntary associations were of course legal and recognized the rights of people to join any organization they might think worthwhile.

Before the 1930s, unions operated as one might expect. They used the threat of withholding the labor services of their members as a means of securing better employment contracts.[86] In the case of jobs that required a large amount of skill to perform well, such a threat was useful in bringing an otherwise reluctant employer to the bargaining table to negotiate a better deal for the workers involved. As such, the union had an interest in promoting the skills of its members so that a threatened strike might carry greater weight. Nonetheless, the property owning employer was always free not to negotiate in such circumstances but to make job offers to other potential workers as best he could.

In practice, the activities of unions typically went beyond this kind of activity. In addition to merely withholding the labor services of its members, unions have typically also threatened the use of violence against an employer's property and against other potential workers who might be willing to accept job offers to replace union workers. The threatened violence is made via the

---

[86] For a good essay on the right of union members to strike, see Charles W. Baird, "On the Right to Strike," *The Freeman*, (Irvington, NY: Foundation for Economic Education, October 1990).

picket line and the use of verbal abuse against replacement workers. In some cases, these threats of violence erupt into actual acts of violence against people and property. Prior to the 1930s, it was the duty of the governmental authorities to intervene in such cases to secure the order and peace of the community by putting down such uprisings using whatever means might be necessary. In other words, the purpose of government was to protect people and their property against the threats of unions and their members. To the extent that unions engaged in such threats and actual acts of violence against people they put themselves at odds with the law and thus invited the force of government to be used against them.

It is perhaps needless to say that on such occasions when the force of government is needed to put down the violence associated with a union's strike, a rift in community relations is sure to follow. Indeed, the resulting struggle to regain and maintain control typically results in the destruction of much personal property and even the loss of life. Those who suffer from such losses are likely to hold onto feelings of indignation directed at those whom they hold responsible for the violence regardless of whether or not those feelings are rightly directed.

A case example will be useful to illustrate this point. In 1892, a strike erupted into violence in Homestead, Pennsylvania.[87] The strike was organized by union workers against a steel plant owned by Andrew Carnegie while Carnegie was on vacation in Europe. The strike was brought on as negotiations on a new employment contract stalled. Carnegie's manager in charge at that time, Henry Clay Frick, hired Pinkerton agents to protect the property of the plant and had taken various actions for the purpose of securing the property against any union attack. Union workers responded with violence against these agents and against any worker that was

---

[87] See Cheri Goldner, "The Homestead Strike 1892," *American Culture Studies "Computing for ACS" course,* Spring 1997. The article can be found at www.bgsu.edu/departments/acs/1890s/carnegie/strike.html.

willing to cross their picket line. The violence eventually resulted in the deaths of three Pinkerton agents and seven workers. In addition, many other people were wounded in the episode and property was destroyed. To restore order to the community the Pennsylvania National Guard had to be called out.

The entire affair left a good many people bitter. A substantial portion of this bitterness was directed toward Andrew Carnegie. While it might have been nice if Carnegie had avoided the confrontation by appeasing the union leaders, he was hardly to be blamed for the violence, the destruction of property, and the deaths of the people in the Homestead strike. In truth, the plant did not belong to the workers and they had no right to it or to the jobs they held there apart from the mutual willingness of Carnegie to provide those jobs to them on terms that he found acceptable. Given their unwillingness to continue their employment on the condition of the terms offered to them, Carnegie and his representatives were acting fully within their authority and right to seek replacement workers. The fact that union members responded with violence to such a situation means that they were the ones responsible for the destruction and the deaths that resulted from their actions. Nevertheless, many people blamed Carnegie. Why?

There are perhaps a lot of reasons for this. One reason for such misdirected blame is the observable difference in wealth between those who own factories and plants and those who are hired to work in them. In the case of Carnegie, it was obvious that he was very wealthy and those who worked for him in his plants were not. As such, people tended to sympathize with those who had less wealth and tended to believe that those with more should be the first to make an accommodation. But such sympathies miss the point. Carnegie made his fortune by offering significant economic opportunities to a whole host of other people. His activities benefited his customers as well as his employees. His development of successful business ventures overflowed not only to himself, but to those who bought and used his products. In an effort to maintain a good standing in the market, he always had to consider the markets for both the products he sold as well as those in which he bought resources for production. As long as he believed that he would be able to attract workers of sufficient skill to produce the product of sufficient quality to maintain his position in the market without increasing the amount he paid for labor he was free to attempt to do so. No one had a claim against him for doing this and the use of violence against him at this point was simply not justified. But the presence of jealousy, envy, and greed that exists in the human heart is not likely to see things that way. In fact, such passions are the reason that people tend to shape their views of such circumstances with a favorable prejudice towards the poorer members of this world and against those of greater economic means.

Labor policy in America took a dramatic turn during the 1930s with a series of laws passed during the New Deal era of Roosevelt. These laws provided unions with special legal privileges that were denied to people generally. In fact, these pieces of legislation effectively launched an attack on private property and the right of people to contract voluntarily on terms they find agreeable. One of the first and most significant of these acts is known as the National Labor Relations Act of 1935 (also known as the Wagner Act). In effect, this legislation forced employers to bargain with the unions of its employees in good faith and set guidelines that employers had to follow. To enforce the terms of the act, the legislation created the National Labor Relations Board which was granted some quasi-judicial authority to intervene in labor disputes. The board was granted the authority to investigate complaints against employers, to issue orders against them, and to seek the enforcement of its orders in federal courts. In essence, the act sanctioned the ability of unions to undercut the property rights of employers by forcing them to negotiate with them when they might not otherwise be inclined to do so. In addition, it allowed them to stage veiled threats of violence against replacement workers by sanctioning picket lines so long as they did not actually result in violence. Of course, the veiled threat is always the first step toward actual violence and when unions failed to achieve their purposes they typically resorted to such violence. The only difference in the actions of unions after the passage of this act when compared to their actions beforehand was that union leaders and their members were more emboldened than ever in their use of such violence.[88] This is the natural result of granting anyone a special political privilege under the law. In truth, it amounted to the government's abdication of its responsibility to equally protect the property and liberty of all Americans.

The NLRA was later modified by the Taft-Hartley Act of 1946 and by the Landrum-Griffin Act of 1959. Nevertheless, it remains the cornerstone regulation providing unions a privileged legal position. The result of this change in the law, away from the equal protection of life, liberty, and property of all Americans, toward the establishment of special privileges for unions marked a substantial change in legal thought. It opened the door for a host of lawsuits and countersuits in courts as various people and interest groups attempted to use the law for their own interests.[89] The result has been a greatly confused market for labor with an ever expanding list of rules and regulations governing employment. In the most recent times, the efforts of the unions have been thwarted to some degree. Nevertheless, they remain active lobbyists in Washington and press hard for legislation that will advance their agenda. Among the things they tirelessly strive for are rules, regulations, and laws that price competitive laborers out of the market. In that regard they push for high tariff rates on foreign imports, strict quotas on the number of allowable imports into the country, and higher minimum wages.

---

[88] For an excellent discussion of some of the actual practices of union members and the violence they have participated in see Clarence Carson, *The War on the Poor*, (Phenix City, AL: American Textbook Committee, 1991), pp. 117-157.

[89] For an excellent discussion of the good purpose of government in society, see Frederic Bastiat, *The Law*, (Irvington, NY: Foundation for Economic Education).

The Establishment of Minimum Wage Laws

Hand-in-hand with the government's grant to unions of the requirement forcing employers to bargain collectively, was the establishment of the minimum wage. The first attempt at a system wide minimum wage was found in a provision of the National Industrial Recovery Act of 1933. Actually, this act had also attempted to provide unions with greater bargaining clout as well. However, these provisions of the legislation were struck down as unconstitutional by the Supreme Court. Following this set back, Roosevelt began looking for a means to undercut the Court's decisions on his New Deal policies. To do so he looked to change the makeup of the Court by increasing the number of justices. This action was strongly opposed, but it turned out not to be necessary as Roosevelt was able to make enough likeminded judicial appointments to change the outcome of the Court decisions that were being made. By 1937, the makeup of the Court had been sufficiently altered so that the push for additional New Deal legislation went forward without the worry that such legislation would later be ruled unconstitutional. In this new legal environment, Congress passed the Fair Labor Standards Act in 1938 which established a nationwide minimum wage. The act was very popular among the unions which have typically supported the ready increase of it.

The economics of the minimum wage is straight forward enough. The law establishes a price floor for unskilled labor. Like all price floors, economic theory predicts that the establishment of an effective minimum wage will lead to surplus labor, or unemployment, among unskilled workers. Indeed, when one examines the data, one finds that unemployment rates among teenagers and the less educated people are higher than the average rate of unemployment in the economy.[90] That is, low skilled laborers are the least employable workers in the nation.

Given these facts, it is interesting that labor unions

---

[90] This fact is borne out by the U.S. Department of Labor statistics on employment.

should be such strong lobbyists for increasing the minimum wage. In effect, the minimum wage hinders the economic opportunities available to those who need employment opportunities the most. Why do unions support this law? The reason is because it works to their benefit. In effect, the law is intended to price a competitive form of labor out of the market place. In turn, this gives unions a better position from which to bargain with employers for higher wages for their members. The reality that this is true can be understood first by asking the question, how many union members make minimum wage? The answer, of course, is none. Unions represent workers who possess significant skills and who command wages significantly higher than the legal minimum in labor markets. Therefore, an increase in the minimum wage does not have any direct bearing on union members. Rather, such minimums directly impact the unskilled labor market.

To clarify the reason for union support for this kind of law, suppose I wanted to contract with a lawn service to maintain my yard. Suppose further that I had contacted two such firms and received the following bids. Imagine that one service is owned and operated by an individual who had been in the business for a good many years and had a reputation of excellence and skill in the delivery of the service and that he was asking $40 weekly to take care of my yard. Imagine that the other service is operated by two teenage boys who are trying to break into the business and they are willing to do the job for $30 per week. If I believe that the two younger workers will be able to deliver a similar product to that of the lawn care professional, I may well decide to contract with the less experienced but cheaper teenage boys. However, suppose that lawn care professionals everywhere band together to lobby Congress for the passage of a law requiring buyers of lawn care service to pay a minimum price for such services. They might use a litany of rhetorical reasons to support such a law. For example, they might say that no one person can make a living providing lawn care services unless he is paid a minimum of $25 per yard, per week for it and anyone who pays less than that is exploiting such an employee. If the professionals are effective in their lobbying efforts and a law is passed, then by law the two teenagers could not bid less than $50 per week to provide their lawn service. In effect, the law limits their freedom to contract with me and prices them out of the market. If I still wish to contract for a lawn care service, I'll be forced to negotiate with the professional. The only difference will be that now he will likely ask for more than $40 per week to provide his service. In essence, this is what the unions are doing when they push for higher minimum wages.

Despite the overwhelming logic of the case against the minimum wage law, and despite the abundant evidence to support this logical conclusion, lawmakers have continually voted to increase the minimum over the years. The need to do this can be understood when we factor in the impact of inflation. As the Federal Reserve pursues a general policy of monetary inflation, it reduces the effectiveness of the legal minimum because the actual market clearing wage for unskilled labor is driven up by the inflation, other things equal. As a result, the unions continually advocate and lobby for increases in the minimum wage in order to secure the desired bargaining benefits that can be derived from it. Over the years, the minimum wage has increased from $0.40 per hour to its current level of $5.85.[91] In recent years elected officials sought for an increase in the minimum. Whether or not this happens is uncertain, but the trend suggests that it is only a matter of time before such an increase is imposed. Nonetheless, from the standpoint of workers and consumers generally speaking, the best policy would be the elimination of the law altogether.

Other Labor Issues

From the discussion of the minimum wage law, and the

---

[91] Some states have actually set the minimum above this number and it will likely be raised again nationally in the future.

privileged position that has been granted to unions, it should be clear that the government has embarked on the establishment and maintenance of policies that insure higher rates of unemployment than would exist otherwise. "Real wage rates can rise only to the extent that, other things being equal, capital becomes more plentiful. If government or the unions succeed in enforcing wage rates which are higher than those the unhampered market would determine, the supply of labor exceeds the demand for labor. Institutional unemployment emerges."[92] If the government maintains its commitment to these kinds of policies, there may well be calls for more intervention in the market to alleviate the hardships of the unemployment that its own policies created. In fact, that is what the government has done. To address higher rates of unemployment, the government has created unemployment insurance, set itself up as the main arbiter in labor disputes, spent large sums of money on public works projects in the name of creating jobs, and put greater pressure on the Federal Reserve to expand the money supply more rapidly. All of this activity is done to alleviate the unintended consequences of the previous government action, and it all produces a myriad of additional negative consequences.

Government mandated unemployment insurance first came into existence with the passage of the Social Security Act of 1935.[93] In addition to the well-known retirement benefits associated with this legislation, this New Deal legislation forced some employers to pay a tax to provide unemployment benefits for their workers. The tax was levied as a percentage against the size of a company's payroll. Because of the specifications of the law, there were underlying incentives that prompted state governments to draft their own unemployment insurance laws as well. As a result, they subsequently got into the business of

---

[92] Ludwig von Mises, "Unemployment," *The Freeman*, (Irvington, NY: Foundation for Economic Education, September 1981).

[93] For a good summary of unemployment insurance and its economic impact, see George Leef, "Unemployment Compensation: The Case for a Free Market Alternative," *Regulation*, Winter 1998, pp. 19-26.

providing unemployment benefits. In its initial form, such insurance was made available to about a third of all employees. However, in time the percentage of people covered has grown as additional legislation extended the coverage. While the provision of unemployment insurance varies from state to state, it is safe to say that such coverage only came about via federal rule making which aimed at usurping the right of free negotiation of contract between employers and employees.

One interesting feature of the existence of such insurance is that it tends to increase the duration of unemployment by making the circumstances of unemployment less severe. Indeed, in the early nineties, in the latter part of the Bush administration, Congress passed an extension of the period of time that someone could legally receive unemployment compensation. At the time the nation was in the midst of a recession and the act was intended to alleviate some of the hardships being suffered by the unemployed. Nonetheless, shortly after the passage of the act, the unemployment rate rose which brought about media reports discussing the escalation of the recession. In truth, the real reason for the increase was owed primarily to the extension of the time that unemployment insurance could be paid. This follows from the realization that the economy was already emerging from the recession and a new level of economic growth was at hand at the same time that the extension was made. Nonetheless, unemployment rates rose. Put simply, if you pay people to be unemployed, you will have more people unemployed.

Despite this known economic relationship, some proponents of mandated government unemployment insurance argue that it serves to stabilize the economy by replacing some income of those left unemployed in an economic downturn.[94] However, as we saw in the earlier chapter on monetary policy, a business downturn is primarily spawned by an earlier monetary expansion that results in numerous capital investments that

---

[94] Ibid.

cannot be economically successful in the long run. As such, the payment of unemployment insurance would provide workers in such industries with the ability to wait longer for a possible return to work in industries that might not have a real economic future. As a result, such compensation would actually prolong a recession by discouraging the kind of resource mobility that is needed to return the economy to full employment.

The fundamental problem with government unemployment insurance is that it undercuts the age old private methods of providing for one's financial security: personal savings plans and private insurance. Indeed, if it were not for the government's meddling into the personal affairs of its citizenry, they would have every incentive to pursue such private options as might make sense in their individual situations. However, to the extent that the government imposes taxes upon them, they are limited in their abilities to do so and are left to rely upon a one size fits all bureaucratic offering.

Since the government's initial foray into manipulating and regulating labor markets, other issues have surfaced that provided new opportunities for intervention. Chief among these was the issue of racial discrimination. The aftermath of the Civil War in the United States, and the subsequent policies of reconstruction had greatly alienated the races in the South. Over the course of many years, many Southern states adopted segregation laws that prevented blacks from enjoying the freedom of association that was a fundamental principle upon which the nation was founded.[95] These laws prevented black people from being able to freely enter into some mutually agreeable contracts, from participating freely in certain everyday practices that whites took for granted, from being able to adequately seek legal redress in courts of law, and from voting. These laws distorted justice and treated blacks unequally before the law. This injustice

---

[95] For a good presentation on the issue surrounding affirmative action, see Walter E. Williams, "Affirmative Action Can't Be Mended," *The Cato Journal*, Spring/Summer 1997. I am summarizing here some of the issues he deals with in that article.

brought about a civil rights movement that rightly aimed to repeal these laws so that all people, regardless of their skin color, would be treated equally under the law.

In time the civil rights movement was successful at eliminating these laws. However, rather than rejoicing in the success of the abolishment of these laws of injustice, the movement set its sights on gaining political advantage for those who had been made to suffer under the those laws. This was done by seeking legal privilege for those who had been made to suffer. What the civil rights leaders began to push for after the abolition of segregation laws was for new laws, known widely as affirmative action laws, which would mandate that certain special privilege be directed towards those who had suffered under the older laws. Essentially, what the leaders of the movement wanted was for government to pass laws that would force others to hire black people, to accept them into their clubs, and to provide a list of other privileges simply because they happen to have a particular color of skin.

Unfortunately, the only means available for government to grant this kind of privilege is to impose costs on others through increased taxes. The government simply has no means of providing such privilege apart from this because it does not have any resources of its own. Therefore, to provide the legal benefits desired, the government had to pass new laws based solely upon race. In effect, these new laws and policies would treat people differently under the law which was the problem the earlier movement had sought to alleviate. Put succinctly, it had to inflict injustice on some by establishing laws that provide unequal treatment of people before the law. Inequality would be based merely upon the color of one's skin. Only in this case, the table would be turned against whites and anyone else thought to reside in the majority.

The main problem with such a result is that it extends injustice under the law in a new direction and this can only end in greater strife between people as the new victims of the legal code seek redress. In his essay, "The Law," Frederic Bastiat dealt with the problem of unjust laws and their remedy. In that article he wrote:

> Law is the organization of the natural right to legitimate self-defense; it is the substitution of collective force for individual forces, to act in the sphere in which they have the right to act, to do what they have the right to do; to guarantee security of person, liberty, and property rights, to cause *justice* to reign over all... It is in the nature of men to react against the iniquity of which they are victims. When, therefore, plunder is organized by the law for the profit of the classes who make it, all the plundered classes seek, by peaceful or revolutionary means, to enter into making of the laws. These classes, according to the degree of enlightenment they have achieved, can propose two different ends to themselves when they thus seek to attain their political rights: either they may wish to bring legal plunder to an end, or they may aim at getting their share of it. Woe to the nations in which the masses are dominated by this last thought when they, in their turn, seize the power to make the law![96]

This is precisely what has happened. The victims of the segregation laws have now pursued laws that extend injustice in a whole host of new directions. Moreover, they have invited people throughout the nation to attempt to identify themselves as being victims of some kind of wrong in order to seek similar kinds of legal redress. The damaging effects of such efforts will inevitably lead to the greater damage of society. The only thing that government can do to end injustice caused by unjust laws is to eliminate the laws themselves. Any attempt to right the balance of justice by creating new laws that tip the scales in the other

---

[96] Frederic Bastiat, *Selected Essays on Political Economy*, (Irvington, NY: Foundation for Economic Education, 1995), pp. 52&55.

direction can only perpetuate and spread injustice in new directions.

Despite this truth, our government has been open to passing laws that further limit the freedoms of Americans to contract and associate with others on terms that they find agreeable to them. As a result, the government has invited whole new classes of individuals to lobby for additional laws aimed at addressing supposed issues of injustice that they face. For instance, women's groups have banded together to claim that women have been made to suffer under certain discriminatory practices of employers and that government intervention is needed to protect their interests. In this effort, feminist organizations have pressed for comparable worth laws that would set government standards on what someone should be paid to perform a particular kind of job on the basis that these legal standards would end the discrimination.

Regrettably, these laws only insure discrimination because they upset market equilibriums. In the free market, what a person commands as a wage rate depends on a whole list of different factors. Included among these factors is the likely permanence of the worker in the labor market since the amount that potential employers would invest in training someone would depend upon the likelihood that they would recoup such investments through the continued employment of that person. Traditionally, women have chosen to move in and out of the labor market in order to pursue other interests, namely raising families, and this fact tends to lower the wage rates women command generally speaking. Of course, women who prove their commitment to work, and display abilities for the work, are more likely to receive the training that they desire, and, hence, are more likely to command higher wages. If we ignore this fact and impose governmental standards on pay, it is most certainly going to work against most women. Those not willing to make the permanent commitment to work will generally find employers less willing to take a chance by hiring them.

Consider a free market for labor for a moment and this

will become more evident. In a free market, all employers compete with one another in their efforts to attract suitable workers. If an employer desired to hire people on the basis of some discriminatory prejudice, he would have to pay a premium to do so. That is, it would lead to a wage differential based on that prejudicial preference. However, suppose one employer ignored the discriminatory practices of others. He would be able to hire quality employees at a fraction of what other employers were paying to maintain the prejudice. As a result, he would have a distinct advance over his competition as he could sell his product at a lower price in the market and capture a greater share of it. In this way, he would drive his competitors out of business as long as they chose to maintain their prejudicial viewpoint. Faced with such a situation, it is highly unlikely that they would do so. In this way, all other things being equal, the wages of the class of people originally discriminated against would rise while the wages of the favored class would fall.

Alternatively, suppose that government attempts to intervene in the situation by mandating prices for labor services. The first thing to note is that bureaucrats are not able to distinguish between wage differentials that have an economic basis and those that arise from discrimination. As a result, their impositions are likely to create a series of shortages and surpluses of labor in various sectors of the economy. Any time such shortages and surpluses occur the decision to hire will be based on something other than the economics of the situation. Thus, such governmental intervention is most likely to make various forms of prejudicial discrimination systematic.

What we learn from all of this is that government has greatly expanded its influence over labor markets in America and that has had certain consequences. Namely, the policies of the federal government have distorted labor markets, increased unemployment especially among the least skilled members of society, and promoted prejudicial hiring practices. Despite this, government officials continue to clamor for new ways to meddle in the private affairs of employers and employees.

Chapter 8: Welfare Policy

The Socialistic Concept Behind all Welfare Policies

The welfare state in the United States was primarily birthed in the legislation of the New Deal. While there were numerous laws enacted to foster the development of the welfare state, the cornerstone piece of legislation was the Social Security Act of 1935. In essence, the driving idea behind establishing and expanding a welfare state is the notion that it is a function of government to insure the adequate means of life for all people who live under its rule. That is, government is viewed as being a supreme parent endowed with the ability to provide for the needs of the people under its care. In reality, the welfare state arises when the government adopts a wide array of laws and policies aimed at the vast redistribution of wealth and income. Essentially, it is the situation in which the governing authorities use the power of their positions to expropriate the property of some for the purpose of giving it to others. This practice is largely associated with democratic government because within this system politicians can best gain political advantage by promising to provide benefits for their constituents. It must be noted of course that such promises can only be kept by violating the property rights of some people by employing the coercive force of government to confiscate their property by taxation.

To understand how the welfare state flourished in the U.S. since the 1930s, one must also understand the nature of socialism and its spreading impact in our world. As a philosophy of political control, socialism was developed by various intellectuals in Europe during the eighteenth and nineteenth centuries. The ideas promoted by these intellectuals were especially prominent in France. Among the accepted ideas of the socialists was the notion that the value of something was the result of the amount of labor embedded in it. On the basis of

118 • Unmasking the Sacred Lies

this theory, Karl Marx argued that workers in free market economies were being exploited to the extent that their wages fell below the revenues raised from selling the products they produced. That is, any payment to the owners of capital or land was considered illegitimate. Therefore, it was thought that such payments should be eliminated in order to usher in a utopian society. Thus the idea that was central to socialist planning was the belief that through exercising political control in the right way, a government could bring about heaven on earth. For this reason, Marx advocated a revolutionary overthrow of capitalistic governments and the abolition of property rights because he saw these institutions as being the source of the problems that people faced.

As an alternative to revolution, some advocates of socialism argued that the utopian dream they envisioned could be had through the process of gradualism. Rather than calling for the revolutionary overthrow of the existing governmental powers, these thinkers argued that socialism could be had piecemeal by working continuously within the confines of the existing governmental structures in democratic societies. Thus, they began to advocate new government programs that would compromise the rule of property right law in subtle ways at the margin. To promote such policies, the social reformers sought to focus people's attention on the benefits that these programs would provide while ignoring or minimizing the costs. In addition, such programs were sold as being a sort of philanthropic enterprise. For example, socialists were quick to argue for the establishment of government schools to provide for the delivery of free public education. They proclaimed that such education was an essential right of the individual and that everyone ought to have it without regard to how it would be paid for.

Unfortunately, the provision of any good or service cannot be conceived of as a right on equal par with the protection of life, liberty, and property because such provision cannot be universally extended on equal terms. While a government can conceivably commit itself to the protection of each individual's property on equal terms, it cannot guarantee the provision of a good on the same terms because it does not have the economic wherewithal to provide any good. As far as institutions are concerned, governments are of the beggar sort and are totally dependent on the resources of the governed to be viable institutions. Therefore, if a government attempts to engage in the parental enterprise of providing some good for public consumption, it must obtain the resources to support the effort by taking them from someone. However, to do this would mean that the institution essentially violates its main reason for existence, namely the protection of people generally speaking.

Nevertheless, socialists played upon the general sentiments of people to promote the idea that it was possible for government to be an institution of charity in society. Once again, it is not possible for democratic governments to serve this purpose because such institutions do not have any resources from which they might be charitable. True charity always involves a voluntary choice on the part of the person extending the charity. Therefore, for one person or group of people to show charity to others, they must first possess the resources needed that they can then give away. But, in fact, all democratic governments are fully dependent upon various means of taxation to secure the resources to fund their operations. Therefore, a democratic government cannot give away anything to anyone that was not first taken from someone else. And, since taxes are collected by using force, such actions effectively undermine property right law in those societies where these programs are adopted. As a result, voluntary choice is eliminated when a democratic government mandates a new redistribution program whether the goods being provided are education, healthcare, housing, old age pensions, or food. In each case, these goods can only be given away by the government to the extent that they have first been taken away from someone else.

Just the same, the socialists successfully played upon the sympathies of people to gradually expand the array of welfare

programs in the western nations with democratic governments.
At each step, the fundamental goal was to abolish property rights.
In their thinking, this kind of abolition of the rule of property
right law would amount to extending social justice in society
because it was thought that such rule gave rise to the exploitation
of labor. Sadly, this mentality is wholly misguided. In fact, by
undercutting the rule of property right law, these programs have
allowed politicians and various assorted factions in society the
opportunity to live at the expense of others. In essence, they live
like leaches. As a result, they have tended to hinder economic
prosperity thus promoting greater economic hardship in society.

Social Security: The Cornerstone of Welfare Policy in America

The classic example of socialistic redistribution in the
United States is also the nation's centerpiece welfare state policy.
The Social Security System was established in 1935 for the
purpose of providing monetary benefits for the aged in America.
From the beginning, the program provided those benefits by
redistributing money via a payroll tax. Unlike a private
retirement plan, Social Security relied wholly on redistributed tax
dollars as its means of funding. In essence, the government
created an enormous pyramid scheme and forced the citizens of
America to participate. The long term effects of this program are
exactly the same as the long term effects of all such Ponzi
schemes. A Ponzi scheme is named after Charles Ponzi who was
known as the Boston Swindler. In the early part of the twentieth
century, Ponzi, an Italian immigrant, duped a large number of
people by guaranteeing a 50 percent return on an investment in
ninety days. Initially, Ponzi kept his promise by using the funds
of later investors to make good on earlier commitments.
Actually, making these payments served as excellent advertising
for his plan and many people lined up to "invest" their funds. In
reality, Ponzi had no means of making good on his promise
because he had no business enterprise that could actually
generate this return. In fact, he simply took the money that

people were investing and deposited it in accounts under his own name with local banks. These accounts generated meager returns of around five percent per year. As a result, the more money that investors deposited with him, the larger the deficit between what he possessed in assets and what he promised to pay his investors. However, as long as the number of people that were being duped was increasing fast enough, Ponzi was able to make good on earlier commitments and this fueled greater interest in his supposed business. Eventually, authorities' suspicions were confirmed and it became clear that the scheme was a fraud. When the news finally hit, large numbers of investors were left holding worthless paper.

Social Security is in reality set up in essentially the same fashion. It relies on the payments made by later generations to pay out benefits to earlier generations. As such, it suffers from the same kind of fraud in financing that Ponzi's scheme suffered. Namely, early beneficiaries receive large rewards at the expense of those who come into the plan later. In time, all such plans fail to financially provide what was promised. This has been the exact pattern of Social Security since its inception. Early beneficiaries did quite well in the program. However, as the numbers of those receiving benefits continued to climb, so too did the payroll tax rates needed to fund them. At this point in time, the outlook for young employees today is bleak. The prospect that they might enjoy any compensation for the taxes that they will pay is highly unlikely given that the program faces such a large unfunded liability over the course of the next thirty years. In effect, the Social Security System is an immense system of income redistribution from later to earlier generations.

When it was originally established, the payroll tax imposed was set at one percent of the first $3,000 a person earned matched by the employer. In other words, the tax amounted to two percent of the first $3,000 in earnings or $60 per year. The program's first recipient was a woman named Ida Fuller. Mrs. Fuller retired in 1940 having paid a total of $44 in payroll taxes. She then began to draw social security benefits which totaled almost $21,000 for the 35 years she lived after retiring.[97] Clearly, Mrs. Fuller made out quite well. A private investment of $44 in the marketplace would not have provided a rate of return sufficient to provide the benefits that she enjoyed.

However, things are quite different today. Most young people seriously doubt that they will ever receive a single dime in benefits from Social Security even though they expect to pay high payroll taxes over the course of their working lives.[98] Their fears are not unfounded. Because of demographic changes in the makeup of the population, the number of people working who are able to provide the benefits of one retiree has been declining and is expected to decline even further in the future. According to the Social Security Administration's own report, there were 3.3 workers per beneficiary in 2003 and this number was expected to drop to 2.7 by 2015 and to 2.2 by 2030.[99] This decrease means that each worker will have to pay more in payroll taxes if the system is to make good on the benefits it has promised future retirees. However, at some point higher taxes become an increasingly unlikely policy option.

This trend is not new. It has been ongoing since the start of the program. This fact, coupled with the extension of the program to provide new and increased amounts of benefits, has meant that payroll taxes have had to be increased steadily over the history of Social Security's existence. For the year 2004, the payroll tax rate for disability and survivors benefits stands at 12.4 percent for the first $87,900 in earnings.[100] That means the maximum tax has increased to $10,899.60 as compared to $60 when the program was first instituted. Adjusted for inflation, the initial payroll tax amounted to only $457.59. Thus, even after such adjustment is made, it is clear that this tax has risen

---

[97] Walter Williams, "Social Security: Our Pleasure, Our Children's Disaster," *National Minority Politics,* May 1994, pg. 19.
[98] Peter G. Peterson, *Will America Grow Up Before It Grows Old?,* (New York: Random House, 1996), pg. 4.
[99] Social Security Administration, 2003 Annual Report of the Board of Trustees of the Federal Old-Age and Survivors Insurance and Disability Trust Funds.
[100] Ibid.

dramatically over the years. To be sure, additional legislation over the years has significantly increased the kind of benefits paid out by the system. Nonetheless, the increase in the amount of taxation associated with Social Security is dramatic in spite of these changes. Not only is this the case, but the agency's own estimates demonstrate that higher tax rates would be needed to make good on the promised benefits of future retirees.

These facts have increasingly led to calls for the privatization of the system into individual retirement accounts. However, such calls have met strong resistance politically. One reason for that resistance is associated with the so-called Social Security Trust Fund. Even though the program operates fundamentally as a pay as you go system, it was established in such a way as to pay out benefits as if they were coming out of a trust fund. Initially, the difference in the year that the program was established and the year the first beneficiary was paid allowed for the development of this "fund" and this gave the program the illusion that it was operated like a private retirement savings plan. Regrettably, that is not true. Any money coming into the system that is not paid out as benefits is lent to the Treasury. Nonnegotiable bonds are placed in the Trust Fund. The problem with this approach is that it ignores the essence of the liability that is being created by one part of government against itself.

To understand the problem with this, suppose that a person just received a pay increase of $500 per month and decided to establish his own personal automotive trust fund for the purpose of buying an automobile at some future date. Rather than purchasing financial instruments issued by other individuals, suppose our person cleverly decides to loan himself the money. Each month he loans himself $500 and signs a bond promising to pay $500 at 8 percent interest annually. He then spends the money as he likes and places the bond in his automotive trust fund lockbox. Over the years he watches the number of bonds accumulate in his lockbox. However, his plan will prove to be of little actual value when it comes time for him to buy an automobile because in order to pay off the bonds he must either cut back on his consumption of other things or find some new sources of income. If neither of these options is feasible, the only other options would be for our individual to borrow the money to buy the car from someone else or to give up on the idea of buying a car altogether. There simply are no other options because there never was any real savings to draw on for the purpose of buying automobiles.

This is exactly how the Social Security Trust Fund has operated over the years. The existence of this so called trust fund has simply been a matter of illusion. This fact became apparent relatively soon after the creation of Social Security and this led to Congressional legislation that bumped up payroll taxes to pay the program's beneficiaries. When tax revenues from the program exceed the amount paid to the beneficiaries in any year, the Treasury simply spends the money on other government programs and places IOUs on account with the agency. Effectively, the government lends the money to itself and promises to pay itself back with interest. However, the only means of payment of these IOUs is for the government to cut its spending on other programs, or to increase its revenues through higher taxes of one kind or another, or to borrow the money from other sources. If none of these options is feasible at the time, the only other thing that could be done is to cut the benefits of the program. Put simply, there are no other options.

The overall direction of the program since its inception has been toward financial ruin. The day of reckoning has continually been postponed by a series of tax increases. These increases have been somewhat offset by increases in benefits offered by the program, but these too have been funded with still higher taxes. In the 1980s, a congressional panel was formed to find a solution the problems in order to right the financial ship of Social Security. What happened as a result of the work of this panel was nothing more than a massive expansion of the program in the same doomed direction. It resulted in the imposition of the most dramatic increases in payroll taxes in the program's history. In 1980, the payroll tax stood at 10.16 percent

on the first $25,900 of earnings or at a maximum tax of
$2,631.44. This included the cost of Medicare which is now paid
for by its own defined tax. By 1990, the tax rate had increased to
12.4 percent on the first $51,300 of earnings for a maximum tax
of $6,361.20. That difference amounts to nearly a one hundred
and forty-two percent increase in the tax in a single decade.

The tax increases imposed during the 1980s set the stage
for an era in which the payroll taxes provided more than enough
revenue each year to pay beneficiaries. However, because of the
way the program is set up, the extra revenue has been used to
finance a whole assortment of new federal programs. Legislators
view the additional revenue from payroll taxes as an easy means
of extending other programs that they desire. To cover over the
underlying accounting fraud being perpetrated against the
American public they invariably make reference to the Trust
Fund. However, they do not count the value of those supposed
bonds as part of the national debt. In truth, the whole process of
using and accounting for the money this way is just smoke and
mirrors. The time is coming when current payroll taxes will fall
short of that needed to pay the promised benefits to retirees.
That date is estimated to be somewhere between 2015-2018
when the baby boom generation begins to retire in large
numbers. At that time, the Social Security Administration will
have to call for the redemption of the bonds and the truth that
they are but a mere fiction will be at hand. Given the
opportunity to look at the numbers, it is impossible to fail to see
the immensity of the problem that looms just a few years out.
Nevertheless, many politicians seem to be very content to
obfuscate the issue. One can only surmise that they have become
so accustom to spending the surplus payroll tax revenue that they
are unwilling to make any effort to face the issue head on today
because it would certainly entail incurring real costs in the here
and now. Politicians seem to be unwilling to face those facts and
so they choose to skate around the issue.

It is hard to see how they can continue to pursue this
kind of head in the sand strategy with respect to Social Security

much longer. That is especially true when one begins to
investigate the projected value of individual retirement accounts.
For example, Fidelity Investments is a company that offers a wide
variety of mutual fund products for investors. The ten year
average return of two such funds is particularly relevant to the
discussion here.[101] One of those funds is a stock index fund
known as the Spartan 500 Index Fund. As its name implies, it is
established in such a way as to hold a wide variety of stocks. Its
average annual return over the past ten years is 11.45%. That is
significant considering that this average takes account of a
substantial market downturn extending from 2000 to 2003. The
other fund worth considering is the Spartan Investment Grade
Bond Fund. During the same time frame it has generated an
average annual return of 7.44% by investing only in high grade
bonds. Using these figures, a portfolio of half invested in the
stock fund and half invested in the bond fund would have
yielded an average annual return of 9.4% in the same ten year
period.

   With this information, we can then make some quick
projections about how well an individual might fare if his payroll
taxes went into his own private account, rather than into the
U.S. Treasury. For instance, consider a person who had an
average annual salary of $45,000 per year from age 25 to 65. If
this person could achieve a 9% return on his portfolio over the
years, his account would grow to $1,885,384 when he turned 65.
At the same rate of return on investment he would be able to
achieve an annual retirement income of $169,685 a year and
never draw down the balance which he could then leave to his
heirs. In other words, he could achieve a retirement income of
nearly four times what he actually made in any year.

   Some might argue that while this may be true for higher
income individuals, the real problem is those who are poor.
However, the numbers are even worse when we consider the

---

[101] The information here was located in Fidelity's web site at www.fidelity.com. The site provides historical returns on the company's products.

poor. For example, consider an individual who earns minimum wage his entire working life. Suppose our low skill worker earns $5.15 per hour, works a 40 hour week, and takes two weeks of unpaid vacation each year. That person would earn an income of $10,300 annually and pay a Social Security tax of $1,277.20 each year. Of course there is not any need to gain a college education to make minimum wage, so we can assume that he will work from age 20 to 65 or 45 years. If this person had his own private account bearing the 9% return, the account balance would grow to $671,627 by the time he was 65. That would provide an annual retirement income of $60,446 which is nearly six times the amount he earned in any year. Once again, this assumes that he maintains the balance of his account and leaves it to his heirs.

Even if the average rate of return on investment is reduced to 7%, the numbers speak volumes against the current Social Security system. In that case, the person earning $45,000 per year for forty years would accumulate financial assets valued at $1,113,964 and this would provide a retirement income of $77,977 without touching the principal. While the amount is clearly less than before, it is nevertheless significantly higher than what he had earned each year of his working life. Likewise, the unskilled worker would accumulate less in financial assets, but these would still provide a better retirement income than had been earned from working. In this case, the account would grow to $364,959 which would generate a perpetual income of $25,547 at the same 7% rate. One thing is certain, neither of the individuals considered here would receive anything close to these amounts from the Social Security system even if it did make good on its promise to pay.

Given this information, one wonders how long the political elite can ignore the inherent problem of the Social Security system. While some have stepped forward to support some sort of minimal privatization efforts, many continue to play upon the fears of current retirees and near term retirees. They also play upon the ignorance of many as to how financial markets function. In the most recent case, opponents of privatization have used the stock market downturn as a reason why privatization of the system is something that should be opposed. In this way, they play upon the financial ignorance of people generally to promote a new kind of fear. This kind of response from people who are certainly in positions to know the facts can only mean that these politicians are quite willing to postpone the day of reckoning to that point in time when the system plunges off the cliff into utter financial ruin. At that point, benefits will be cut, taxes will be increased, and the government will likely borrow large sums of money to keep some semblance of the program afloat. Sadly, all these measures will hinder the potential for Americans to achieve greater economic prosperity for themselves and their children.

Meddling in Health Care

In her book, *Dependent on D.C.*, Charlotte Twight discusses the political process by which the government has steadily usurped control over the nation's health care industry.[102] Like so much of the establishment and the development of the welfare state, the initial political process of change was set in motion as a result of the New Deal policies of the 1930s. As they originally conceived of it, the framers of the Social Security Act initially thought to make national health insurance a part of the legislation. Yet news of this prospect caused the Roosevelt administration to back down from such an effort in order to pass other portions of the act.

Unwittingly, another measure that the Roosevelt administration pressed into law became a pressing force moving the nation towards a third party payment system for health care services and, thus, provided a backdrop for later efforts to nationalize health care. The legislation at issue here was the Revenue Act of 1935. This law amounted to a massive attack on private property by establishing a highly progressive income tax

---

[102] Charlotte A. Twight, *Dependent on D.C.*, (New York: Palgrave, 2002), pp. 1985-234.

scheme that aimed to soak-the-rich. The top marginal tax rate was pushed to 75% which meant that someone being taxed in that bracket would only be able to keep for himself 25 cents out of each additional dollar he earned. Obviously, the incentive to earn more income if one found himself caught in this tax hell was inconsequential.

For this reason, companies began to look for new ways to attract top level executives. One way to lure such individuals was to provide them with tax free perquisites. One such enticement that companies began to offer was comprehensive health insurance that would pay for all of the executive's health care costs. Ordinarily such insurance would not be considered a viable product offering in a market economy. Since the insurance premium would always be greater than expected outlay for routine health care services, it would make no sense for an individual to purchase such a policy on his own. After all, why would someone pay $1.10 for a dollar's worth of health care if he did not have to? Thus the purchase of insurance to cover the costs of routine health care services makes little financial sense on the face of it.

However, this was not an ordinary situation. The high marginal tax rates imposed on top income earners made for an environment in which it made a great deal of financial sense to accept a comprehensive health care package as partial payment for one's labor services so long as the cost of that insurance was not figured into one's taxable income. If a person could pay for health care services with before tax dollars, he could save a great deal of money in purchasing health care even if he was paying $1.10 for a dollar's worth of service. This is true because if the person were in the top tax bracket, he would have to earn $4.00 in income to be able to purchase $1.00 of health care service since he would only be able to keep 25 cents on each additional dollar that he earned. Clearly, the incentive for individuals in high tax brackets to look for opportunities to receive their pay in the form of these kinds of perquisites was high and comprehensive health insurance plans became one means of providing this sort of in-kind payment for labor services.

This situation might not have spawned the proliferation of comprehensive health care plans had the IRS won its case that aimed to force recipients of such in-kind transfers to report the value of them as part of their overall compensation on tax returns. However, the tax agency lost this case in court and these kinds of payment for services began to spread. The growth of these kinds of perquisites was intensified as a result of monetary inflation which tended to push wages higher and, thus, pressed more and more employees into higher tax brackets through the process known as bracket creep. In this way, lower level managers increasingly had a greater interest in obtaining their own nontaxable benefits packages. In time, they became more ubiquitous in corporate America.

The problem associated with the spread of these plans is that they separate the user of health care services from the payer for such services. In essence, the consumer is no longer price conscious about his use of health care and views it as being an essentially free good since someone else is paying. This problem is known as the problem of moral hazard. Rather than conserve the resource as one would normally do if he had to pay for it, the person has no reason to conserve and will attempt to consume services as long as such services are viewed as having some positive value. Therefore, as a result of the proliferation of comprehensive policies, there was a marked increase in the demand for health care. This, in turn, resulted in higher prices for service. Moreover, as the costs of maintaining these comprehensive health insurance plans increased, insurers began to look for ways to limit these costs. In order to cut costs, insurers placed a host of restrictions and limitations on policy holders.

Politically speaking, while the Roosevelt administration initially backed away from its national health insurance proposal, those embracing a socialist worldview continued to press for it even though it continually met strong resistance. As Twight has shown, they brought up proposals for nationalized health care in virtually every congressional session from 1939 into the 1960s. At each step along the way, the advocates for this kind of policy took whatever incremental step that could be achieved along the way. One such step was to establish social security benefit payments for the disabled which came about in 1956. Another major step toward socialized medicine came in 1965 with the establishment of Medicare, a policy that was part of Lyndon Johnson's Great Society programs.

The establishment of Medicare and Medicaid made the federal government the most prominent third party payer for health care services. By doing so, the federal government became an important factor in the health care industry. In essence, having failed to pass legislation to nationalize the nation's health care industry, the socialists in Congress were able to find a back door method which would in time move the nation closer to actually having such a nationalized system. Under the terms of the legislation, the government provided health insurance for the elderly and for qualifying poor people. The impact of this program was to separate more consumers of health care services from the payment for those services thus dramatically increasing the demand for health care in the same way that private plans were also doing.

The means of paying for these new programs was split. Medicare was established with parts A and B. Part A of the program provided hospital insurance while Part B provided supplemental insurance. Part A of the program was funded through payroll taxes in the same way as other Social Security benefits while Part B was funded through a combination of premium payments imposed upon the elderly coupled with payments from the federal government's general revenues. As Part A spending escalated, the payroll tax was eventually separated so that now a dedicated payroll tax of 2.9% on income funds the program. Moreover, unlike other payroll taxes, there is no cap on the amount of taxable income. That is, all income is subject to the payroll tax to fund Medicare. The Medicaid program was essentially a straight forward welfare program that aimed to redistribute property to the poor by funding their health insurance through general revenues. Just the same, the combination of these programs greatly extended the third party payment system and promoted an even larger moral hazard problem.

An examination of Table 8.1 will be instructive. In 1950, the majority of expenditures for health care services were borne by private consumers. By 1990, the percentage of health care spending by consumers had dropped from 65.5% to 21.9%. In turn, the percentages paid by private insurers and the government climbed substantially. Following the adoption of the Medicare and Medicaid programs, government spending increased from 22.4% in 1950 to 42.9% in 1990. The impact of this shift in payment for services led naturally to the rapid rise in prices for health care services. In turn, these price increases spawned national concern about the affordability of health care which provided those with socialist leanings with a new opportunity to promote even more government intervention.

Table 8.1 Who is Paying for Health Care			
Fiscal Year	Private	Insurance	Government
1950	65.5%	9.1%	22.4%
1960	54.9%	21.1%	21.8%
1970	40.5%	23.4%	34.4%
1980	28.5%	30.7%	39.6%
1990	21.9%	31.7%	42.9%

This table is based on data taken from Edgar K. Browning and Jacquelene Browning, *Public Finance and the Price System*, (New York: Macmillan, 1987, 3rd edition), page 162 and Stan Liebowitz, "Why Health Care Costs Too Much," Cato Institute Policy Analysis no. 211, June 23, 1994.

During the early part of the Clinton administration, one initiative was to establish mandatory health insurance in the U.S. from which there would be no escape. Everyone would be forced into the system whether they liked it or not. In essence, this effort amounted to nationalized health care with the federal government financing and controlling the delivery of health care services. While the effort fell short politically, it did spawn new legislative efforts that eventually resulted in the passage of the Health Insurance Portability and Accountability Act of 1996 or as it is widely known as HIPAA. While this act was presumably intended to correct for certain problems associated with the third party payment system by making health insurance coverage portable from one employer to another, it was also intended to correct for Medicare fraud. To accomplish this accountability problem, onerous limitations and restrictions were imposed on the medical community which tended to move the nation one step closer to a nationalized system. Indeed, the presence of fraud and abuse of a system that the government created was the result of the flawed policies enacted in an earlier era. Attempting to resolve those problems with further intervention would seem to be an utterly foolish endeavor. Nevertheless, that has been direction that legislation and policy as far as the health care industry is concerned.

One of the serious problems associated with the establishment of Medicare is the rapid increase in expenditures that has been associated with the program. For 1967, the government spent $3.2 billion for this program. By 1970, that amount had more than doubled to $6.8 billion. In the next decade, spending increased to $34.0 billion for 1980. In the years since then, this amount has steadily increased year after year and stood at $274.2 billion for 2003.[103] The growth in spending on this program has been impressive and it does not appear that there is any end to the increases in sight. Indeed, the government's own projections anticipate that Medicare spending will climb to $519 billion by 2010.[104] But this is just the tip of the iceberg as spending on this program is expected to increase even faster once the baby boom generation begins to retire in earnest during the decade following that year. Clearly, if the program is

---

[103] This data is taken from the Congressional Budget Office, *Historical Budget Data*, www.cbo.gov.
[104] This data is taken from the Congressional Budget Office, *Current Budget Projections*, www.cbo.gov.

left unchanged, its costs will continue to escalate rapidly into the foreseeable future. So much is this the case that it is exceedingly unlikely that the government could provide the benefits promised in the future since tax rates would be forced to levels far beyond what the government could actually impose.[105]

Despite the looming crisis, Congress and the president demonstrated their unwillingness to face the facts by adding a new prescription drug plan to the existing Medicare program. According to the testimony of a CBO official, the legislation providing the new drug plan is expected to increase Medicare spending by $395 billion over the next decade from 2004 to 2013.[106] As amazing as it seems, despite all the evidence that the Medicare program is increasingly becoming unaffordable, Congress addresses the issue by adding on a new benefit program which is subsequently praised and signed into law by an eager president. The action makes no sense except for the fact that it is sure to create greater hardships in the future which will undoubtedly be used by socialists as a reason why more government control is needed.

Government Action and Rental Housing

The advancement of the welfare state was enhanced when the federal government involved itself in the housing market. Like much of the expansion the key piece of legislation came about during Roosevelt's New Deal. It was the U.S. Housing Act of 1937. Under the terms if this legislation, the U.S. Housing Authority "was authorized to make long-term loans to local governments to build low-cost housing projects and subsidize rents for low income families."[107] The bill also created the Farm

---

[105] See Chris Edwards and Tad DeHaven, "War Between the Generations: Federal Spending on the Elderly Set to Explode," Cato Institute Policy Analysis no. 488, September 16, 2003.
[106] CBO Testimony of Douglas Holtz-Eakin before the Committee on Ways and Means, U.S. House of Representatives, March 24, 2004. The testimony may be found online at www.cbo.gov.
[107] Clarence B. Carson, *A Basic History of the United States: The Welfare State 1929-1985*, (Phenix City, AL: American Textbook Committee, 1986), pp. 89-90.

Security Administration which was established to provide cheaper mortgage credit for farmers. This latter part of the act was the first step in involving the government in mortgage markets. Today, off budget government agencies virtually control these markets. While much more could be said about the proliferation and impact of these agencies on housing, the focus here will be upon the government's financing of public housing projects.

The emphasis of the federal government loans, and later of the offer of outright grants, to local communities was to eliminate dilapidated houses in urban areas and to replace them with public housing units. Thus, while the federal government was not going to be in the business of actually overseeing the construction and maintenance of these projects, the law did provide the incentive for local governments to create their own housing boards in order to solicit the government for money to fund such projects. Indeed, that is what most communities of any size did.

One interesting aspect of this approach is that it provided local authorities the incentive of pursuing policies that might guarantee the existence of slums that could be pointed to as a reason why the community needed federal dollars for some public housing project since the stated goal of the bill was to replace such housing. One of the best means of creating slums in any urban area is for local authorities to impose rent controls on rental housing. In fact, when the nation entered into World War II, such rent controls became common. Whether the local authorities actually understood the impact of rent controls and were simply using the war as a disguise for imposing such controls because they would give rise to future opportunities to seek federal funding is uncertain and debatable. But, the fact that the imposition of such controls produces slums is not uncertain or debatable and most certainly served to spawn new public housing projects in later years.

Like any price ceiling, an effective rent control sets the price of rental housing below the market rate. Moreover, like all such effective controls, it produces a shortage.[108] Put simply, when local authorities imposed rent controls on rental housing they insured that such housing would be in short supply. In addition, they insured that there would be a reduced incentive for building new rent controlled housing. Of course existing tenants of rent controlled housing initially benefit from such controls, but that in itself becomes problematic. If the benefit that these tenants receive is high, they will maintain their residence far longer than they might have done otherwise. As a result, there will be a misallocation of available rental housing.

Beyond the allocation of rental space, landlords are unreasonably penalized as they are denied the opportunity to lease their own property at the highest value possible. Thus, the profitability of renting such controlled housing is diminished. Furthermore, if the controlled rental rate is sufficiently low, it may not be profitable to properly maintain the property or even remain in the business at all. In such cases, the landlord is stuck with rental housing that he cannot make a profit on. This situation is likely to arise in an environment in which rental rates are permanently fixed while monetary inflation drives prices generally higher. In fact, this is the kind of environment that landlords faced in many cases. As a result of this kind of circumstance many landlords simply abandoned their buildings which deteriorated over time to become new city slums. This was certainly the experience of New York City.

In 1965, Congress created the Department of Housing and Urban Development which is known generally as HUD. This change in direction provided grant money to fund government housing projects. This amounted to an extension of the government's involvement in housing and provided larger amounts of money for developing housing projects. Local city officials used the opportunity to seek large amounts of government money to build large scale public housing projects.

---

[108] For an excellent discussion of rent controls, see Henry Hazlitt, *Economics in One Lesson*, (New York: Crown Publishers, 1979), pp. 127-133.

Many such projects were constructed in cities across the country during this time period. However, by anyone's estimation, these public housing projects have been complete failures. These housing facilities are typically plagued by high crime rates and drug abuse. In addition, they quickly deteriorated and became rapidly the very essence of the slums they were intended to replace. Despite the recognized failure of government housing, proponents remain committed to the notion that federal government funding of such projects is beneficial.

This belief has led to the establishment and proliferation of the most recent program of HUD which is called HOPE VI.[109] The project is also known by several different titles including Housing Opportunities for People Everywhere, the Urban Revitalization Demonstration, or the Urban Revitalization Program. Regardless of what it is called, it is a new effort to use taxpayers' money to fund the government's development of housing. Proponents of the new effort argue that the new program will achieve better success. As Andrew Cuomo announced in one of HUD's press releases, the program's aim is to change "the physical shape of public housing by demolishing severely distressed projects–high rises and barracks-style apartments–and replacing them with garden style apartments or townhouses that become part of their surrounding communities."[110] According to Cuomo, the problem with earlier public housing initiatives was that they were built as "high rises" or as "barrack-style apartments" and for that reason alone they became "severely distressed."

In effect, the basic assumption upon which Cuomo based his support for the new program was that the poverty, crime, and drug abuse in older public housing was the result of a poor architectural choice and that correcting that mistake will alter the outcome. Even on the surface, this sounds dubious at best. Larry

---

[109] For a complete discussion of HOPE VI, see Paul A. Cleveland and R. Chris Frohock, "HOPE VI: HUD's Program of False Hope," *Religion and Liberty*, 12.5, September and October, 2002.

[110] "Cuomo Announces $35 Million HOPE VI Grant to Nashville to Transform Public Housing and Help Residents," (Washington, D.C.: Housing and Urban Development, No.99-169, August 30, 1999).

Keating, who is a professor at the Georgia Institute of
Technology, called the question well when he said, "social
pathologies do not inure in buildings. Destruction of the physical
container does nothing to cure the social ills that may afflict the
residents within..."[111] Despite the obvious fact that social ills stem
from other sources, the new program became law in 1992 as an
effort to do something about the horrid condition of government
housing. It grew out of a recommendation by the National
Committee of Severely Distressed Public Housing which pointed
out the deficiencies of public housing. The report acknowledged
that in many cases government housing was deteriorating and
was poorly managed. As a result, HOPE VI was put forward to
"eradicate severely distressed public housing by the year 2000."[112]
Since the adoption of the program, HUD has spent an average of
$500 to $600 million a year under its heading.

Like most government programs, the aim is to achieve
different results by throwing more money at the problem without
changing the approach. Moreover, as long as government
bureaucrats are willing to toss around taxpayers' dollars, there
will always be plenty of people willing to take them and to sing
the praises of the reason why they are doing so. However, that
does not mean that living conditions of the poor will be
improved. Interestingly enough, a great deal of money spent early
in the program has gone to demolish older public housing
facilities. From 1996 to 2001, HUD awarded 177 demolition
grants to cities in 31 states worth $293.3 million for this purpose.
In the city of Chicago alone, the agency provided some $69
million to destroy 10,654 housing units. Thus far, the agency has
funded the demolition of 44,089 public housing units as part of
its HOPE VI initiative.[113]

After destroying the older buildings, under the HOPE VI

---

[111] Larry Keating, "Redeveloping Public Housing: Relearning Urban Renewal's Immutable Lessons,"
    Journal of the American Planning Association, 66.4, Fall 2000.
[112] *HOPE VI*, (Washington, D.C.: Housing and Urban Development, November 2001).
[113] *HOPE VI: Demolition Grants: 1996-2001*, (Washington, D.C.: Housing and Urban Development,
    November 2001).

heading, funds for new construction are provided. In 2001, $492 million was spent on revitalization grants. This money paid for the construction of new mixed-income housing. To date, the agency has spent $4.55 billion on HOPE VI projects.[114] Unfortunately for the poor, the number of units being constructed is less than the number of units that have been demolished. This means that there is a net loss in the total number of housing units as a result of the program. In addition, a fairly large portion of the new units constructed will be sold to higher income residents. According to proponents, the new design of townhouse units, coupled with new middle class residents, is supposed to be the key to solving the woes of earlier urban housing projects. There is good reason to doubt that this approach to urban development will actually deal with the real problem. In the meantime, many of the urban poor are simply being displaced.

The government's track record in housing is not a good one. Like other products, the production and distribution of housing is best left to the private market. Every person has an immediate interest in finding suitable housing to meet the needs of himself and his family. If people are left to pursue their own interests in this regard, developers of housing projects will always produce and offer units in the market such that the market can clear. Furthermore, charitable organizations are always free to intervene with additional funding for housing if they feel compelled to do so. The combination of private market activities coupled with the charitable activities of people is the best way to insure a housing industry that provides for a housing situation that will invariably improve over time.

---

[114] *HOPE VI: Revitalization National Fact Sheet*, (Washington, D.C.: Housing and Urban Development, November 2001).

Prospects for the Future

As the welfare state has expanded in the United States, so too has the size and scope of the government which is precisely what the socialists wanted. In fact, the federal government is so much larger today than it was a hundred years ago, that it hardly resembles its original makeup as conceived of by the nation's Founders. Today's government boasts a wide array of new departments and new agencies that have each been endowed with the power to meddle in private affairs. From education, to healthcare, to urban housing, to business subsidies, to easy credit for certain kinds of loans, today's government is a complex structure of taxing and spending in a fashion that provides welfare for some by penalizing others.

This kind of busybody meddling in the lives of Americans hinders their ability to care for themselves and their families. At the margin, it drives more and more people to the government's programs in hopes that they might be able to make their financial ends meet. However, those ends would more nearly meet if the high taxes and hindrances of government had not been imposed in the first place.

Chapter 9: Business Policy

Introduction

Since the late nineteenth century the federal government has increasingly expanded its role in the market economy. In the process of expansion, the government offered numerous rationalizations to justify its intervention. The Sherman Antitrust Act of 1890, a significant piece of legislation, marked the beginning of the rapid extension of regulatory control. The rationale for the legislation was that it was needed to curb the development of large-scale business trusts. The reasoning behind this assertion was that large businesses, to the detriment of the American people, were unfairly dominating certain industries.

In more recent times, the assertion has been made, on utilitarian grounds, that the government should intervene to regulate businesses when they operate as so-called natural monopolies. That is, proponents of intervention argue that the government has a prominent role to play in the economy when a firm is classified as a natural monopoly, which is said to exist when the market can accommodate only a single supplier. This situation may occur in a market economy when extensive economies of scale are possible. An economy of scale simply means that a firm can reduce the unit cost of production by producing a larger volume. Therefore, if the demand for the good is relatively small in comparison, it could result in a single firm supplying the market. One firm would continue to grow to reap the economies of larger scale, thus driving competitors from the market. The rationale for government regulation is the belief that it would be useful in keeping prices of such products lower than they would otherwise be.

To secure quality and safety assurances, advocates of government regulation have also rationalized intervention. The thinking behind this assertion is that businesses would take advantage of customers because of the increasing complexities of the products being offered. In other words, since the division of labor and the specialization of resources leads to more localized knowledge, it is argued that government regulators are needed to protect customers from charlatans and quacks who would defraud them of their money otherwise.

These arguments have been widely accepted. However, a thorough analysis reveals some serious flaws in them. The goal of this chapter is to examine the criticisms that can be made against each of these rationales and to offer up alternative explanations of how they developed in the first place. They were essentially political rhetoric, providing some plausible reasons for government intervention, to mask the real special interests that were promoted by the establishment of additional laws and regulations.

Antitrust Laws and Regulatory Control

The impetus for regulatory control over industry in the United States came as a result of the granger movement of the latter part of the nineteenth century. As noted in the earlier chapters on transportation and agriculture, the federal government's meddling in the development of transcontinental railroad lines and farming had led to the rapid expansion of agricultural products and, hence, falling product prices. That fact put pressure on marginal and sub-marginal farmers whose profits were eroded. As so often happens in such situations, the farmers were not able to see the forest for the trees. As a result, looking to the most obvious obstacles that thwarted their success, they identified the threatening high rail rates and large scale agricultural suppliers as the main reason undermining their efforts.[115] In response to this situation, organizations of farmers sprang up to protest the rates they considered too high for

---

[115] For a good discussion of this see, Donald J. Boudreaux and Thomas J. DiLorenzo, "The Protectionist Roots of Antitrust," *The Review of Austrian Economics*, Vol. 6, No. 2 (1993): 81-96.

transporting their goods. In addition, they lobbied government for legislation to hinder large scale enterprises. Blaming the railroads and large business firms for their misfortunes, they began to put pressure on state legislatures to impose controls.

These efforts proved fruitful in some states where such legislation was enacted. This set in motion an effort to secure such control nationwide which led to the Act to Regulate Commerce of 1887. This federal legislation established the Interstate Commerce Commission, which resulted in the federal government's management of rail rates. In effect, the act meant that privately agreed-to contracts were no longer acceptable in the bargaining process for rail transportation services and that federal bureaucrats were authorized to determine what rates were "just and reasonable." Rail service providers, no longer able to engage in offering their services on terms they found most advantageous, were now forced to accept the government's assessment of fairness if they wished to continue in the business.

This initial foray into regulating private enterprise began to spread in numerous directions over time. Indeed, transportation regulation was extended to control trucking and other modes of transport services. In time, regulations were extended to all kinds of different industries. Airlines, banks, electric and other energy companies, telephone companies, and many others have faced various sorts of regulatory control. For the most part, these controls have not served the interest of customers, but rather the interests of the regulated firms. In practice, such regulations as have been imposed have set rates and controlled entry into various forms of business enterprise. In this way government regulation has been a means of cartelizing industries and operating them as state-run monopolies. This kind of practice is essentially the kind of mercantilism Adam Smith exposed as undercutting a nation's wealth. Nonetheless, it was the kind of mercantilism that has been spread widely in the United States.

As discussed in some of the other chapters, some of the trends in regulatory control have abated to a degree. Beginning in the 1970s, economists began to attack in earnest the rhetorical arguments offered in support of regulation. As these attacks have gained ground, there has been a move to deregulate significant numbers of U.S. industries. This has resulted in greater competition and a more robust economic advancement. Nevertheless, regulation of numerous industries poses significant problems.

Although regulation of rates and entry into various industries has been significant in U.S. history, it is also important to consider the impact of antitrust legislation, which followed quickly on the heels of the creation of the ICC when Congress passed the Sherman Antitrust Act in 1890. This legislation provided another means for the federal government to meddle in the economy. Namely, it ceded to the federal government the power to break up large scale enterprises that might be deemed anticompetitive.

The problem with the law is that anticompetitive situations have always been established by governments themselves who use the power entrusted to them to thwart trade. Therefore, ceding power to the government to break up a particularly successful business venture is in essence anticompetitive.[116] Without government power restraining business decision makers, people are always free to engage in any enterprise that might be profitable. The fact that only one firm (or a few large firms) should emerge as the product-provider of choice is hardly the occasion of concern. Nor is it troublesome that the competitive advantages held by such a firm should be bothersome. Rather, what should be of concern is that one or a few companies should be recognized by government as the only legitimate providers of a particular good to the exclusion of any potential entrants. Moreover, it would indeed be troublesome that a business would have to worry about being too successful in the process of competition and that its fortunes should be

---

[116] For an excellent economic analysis of antitrust legislation see Dominick T. Armentano, *Antitrust and Monopoly: Anatomy of a Policy Failure*, (New York: John Wiley & Sons, 1982).

undercut as the result of some arbitrary governmental dictate. Notwithstanding, this is in fact what has occurred as a result of antitrust legislation.

As Thomas DiLorenzo has rightly pointed out, the occasion of the Sherman Act was marked by the rapid expansion of government involvement in supporting various business interests.[117] In the case at hand, it was clear to many observers that Senator John Sherman pressed for the antitrust legislation as a means of securing political cover for his real initiative, which was to increase tariffs. Indeed, that is what he did as he sponsored such a tariff increase shortly after the passage of the Sherman Act. As DiLorenzo showed, the legislation was certainly not popular with the economists of the era who largely decried the law as being arbitrary and anticompetitive.

In fact, that is the essence of the law. Dominick Armentano accurately detailed the problems legal scholars face in attempting to apply the law in practice.[118] This reality is evidenced by the additional legislation that has been passed since the initial law went into effect. Later legislation attempted to clarify the issues pursuant to the antitrust actions. In truth, what these additions to the law did was to attack certain forms of competitive activity.

Competition among producers is an inevitable feature of the market economy. This means that those who wish to sell goods in the market must attract customers. To do so, they must make the customer a better offer than their competitors. This sets in motion a process where businesses are forever searching for new competitive advantages. Moreover, past success is no guarantee of future success.

There are many strategies that might be undertaken to attract customers. One is to cut the cost of production. If an entrepreneur finds a cheaper means of production, he can attract

---

[117] Thomas J. DiLorenzo, "The Origins of Antitrust: An Interest-Group Perspective," *International Review of Law and Economics*, Vol. 5, No. 6 (June 1985) 73-90.
[118] Op. cit.

new customers by offering to sell them the good at a lower price. Another popular strategy is to improve the quality of the product. Still another is to offer some additional product or service with the good which is not offered by the competition. These are a few of the most popular means of business competition. Their employment has resulted in the advancement of better and lowered priced goods and services in societies where free markets have been generally allowed to operate.

Competition, however, imposes a discipline on producers. It is not enough to make a good offer to the customer today. There is no place for complacency. A supplier is never guaranteed that tomorrow's consumers will desire to continue buying its product. They may well decide that something else is better. As a result, businesses must be constantly engaged in making improvements. Because of this pressure, there is always a temptation for producers to seek political privilege to limit competition.[119] This is the motive behind antitrust legislation. Indeed, in the government's recent case against Microsoft, it is clear that complaints against the company originated with its competitors who were losing market share. Thus, the aim of government action was not the protection of customers, but the protection of ineffective and inefficient producers.

Quality and Safety Assurances

It has been commonly accepted that the government should provide adequate quality and safety assurances. On the surface this seems to make some sense. As the economy grows, and becomes more complex, resources become more specialized. As this happens, our own knowledge becomes more and more limited. For example, I am writing this using a computer and a word processing program. However, I am not at all sure how either one actually works. Moreover, if either should fail, I would

---

[119] For a discussion of this see Frederic Bastiat, *Essays on Political Economy*. The book is available online at www.econlib.org.

have to seek immediate help from someone else to solve the problem. This is but one of the many products I use daily which remain somewhat a mystery to me. There are, of course, people who do know about these products, but their knowledge of other things is, like mine, limited.

It is asserted by some that limitations in an individual's knowledge results in a failure of the market, which makes government involvement necessary. Otherwise, so the argument goes, people in a market economy would suffer from the continual abuse of dishonest sellers who use their special knowledge to take advantage of customers. This argument, though, assumes that consumers are never able to discern such dishonesty. It also assumes that they cannot overcome their ignorance by private means.

Neither of these assumptions is valid.[120] We are often painfully aware of being mistreated in the market place and there are many private means of gaining useful information to aid our buying decisions. Everyone is aware of the fact that there are people who will attempt to take advantage of others to promote their own interests. For that reason, we all approach buying decisions with some degree of caution. The amount of caution we use is typically linked to the amount we intend to risk in the consumption decision. If the purchase is small, we take little time and expense to avoid mistakes. If it is large, we take many more precautions.

There are a number of issues that must be sorted out when thinking about this situation. First, fraud has always been understood to be a form of theft. As such, it has always been subject to punishment. In cases where consumers have been defrauded, they do have recourse under the law. To do so, they must prove their case. Although this legal activity will not insure that fraud will be mitigated, the threat of punishment will serve

---

[120] For a good discussion of quality and safety assurances see Daniel B. Klein, "Quality-and-Safety Assurance: How Voluntary Social Processes Remedy Their Own Shortcomings," *The Independent Review*, Vol. II, No. 4 (Spring 1998): 537-555.

to dissuade many from such activities. In addition to the problem of fraud, companies have always been at risk in regards to issues of safety arising from their negligence. Indeed, successful tort litigation promotes certain standards of product safety without the creation and involvement of government agencies since financial liability is a powerful motivator.

A second issue arises from situations where fraud or negligence cannot be proved or where the company simply delivers a poor product or a poor service. In these cases, the market functions reasonably well. From a business standpoint, reputation is especially important because consumers often rely on this information in making buying decisions. Companies go to great lengths to develop good reputations. This is why they develop brand names and promote them. In essence, branding is a promise to the customer of consistent product quality and safety. Such efforts, however, are worthless if the firm is not committed to the promise. When bad news spreads about the firm or its products, its reputation declines. Like most everyone, I can give several examples of ending business relationships when I believed the seller was not offering a good value for the money. I can also attest to occasions when I avoided doing business with a seller based on the advice of someone else.

In addition to word of mouth and personal experience, company reputations are often improved or hindered by information developed in private markets. Information provided by private product testers is common in the free market. For example, *Consumer Reports* is a publication of test results generated by a private testing organization. The success of that publication bears witness to the market's ability to generate consumer information on its own. Beyond this kind of information, various associations and accrediting agencies evolve providing the public with quality-and-safety assurances they seek. For example, the college I teach at is accredited. This certification is often publicized as evidence of the educational quality of the school. The biggest problem that might arise in these efforts occurs when these organizations seek the government's favor.

That is, when they seek legislation requiring all firms in a particular line of industry to seek its certification. Such efforts amount to an attempt to monopolize an industry by obtaining special legal privilege. If those efforts are successful, they will tend to undercut the process by which information is generated and spread.

Herein is the problem of an expanding government role. The market process which improves products tends to be thwarted to the extent that government sets and monitors quality-and-safety assurances. After all, how do government bureaucrats come to know what "the best" products are like? In truth, there is no such thing as "the best" because that is a moving target. Whatever might be the best product or the best practice today might well be the poorer one tomorrow. Producers in the free market engage in a trial and error process looking for what might better serve the interests of their customers. Moreover, in the final analysis, it is the customer that determines what is preferable. However, government involvement presumes that some expert knows that beforehand. This is a significant problem. If this approach is fully implemented, it will result in product stagnation. That is, the situation will arise in which no improvement will be made.

Despite the case for leaving the market alone, federal government involvement has exploded over the course of the twentieth century. The government today operates a host of alphabet soup agencies each assigned with tasks of promoting consumer protection in connection with the production and purchase of a wide variety of products. One can only wonder how long true progress can be made in such an environment.

Chapter 10: Environmental Policy

The Environmental Problem and Property Rights

Human beings have always faced environmental problems of one sort or another. All people, as they provide for their needs, produce waste products. As a result, there has always been a need to dispose of these as efficiently and as effectively as possible. Moreover, it is even better to find useful ways to employ waste products so that they no longer need to be disposed of. Indeed, one way that entrepreneurs have gained market advantage in the past is by finding unique uses for things that other people threw away. Just the same, there have always been waste products. That fact is unlikely to change in the near future. The existence of waste means that human action will invariably produce pollution in some form or fashion and that pollution is likely to impact the quality of life.

In the initial stages of human history, people encountered what amounted to a vast commons. To achieve their ends, people developed resources by employing their own labor and using the materials at hand to build suitable dwellings and to provide food and clothing. This process resulted in personal property. The existence of such property in turn gave rise to the prospect that it could be taken by force from the original owners. This prospect, coupled with the fact that human beings can mutually gain from trade, resulted in the development of communities that provided some protection for one's property along with greater opportunities to trade with others.

It is clear from the history of past civilizations that the issue of defining and protecting property was central to the development of governmental rule. One need only read Hammurabi's code or Moses' Pentateuch to find early expressions of rules governing property rights and trade. However, one potential problem of legal codes is that they can be used to mitigate one's right to personal property instead of protecting it. In fact, legal codes have often been established for the purpose of violating the natural rights of property owners for the benefit of some political elite. Large scale plundering of others has most efficiently been carried out through the ages by the actions of governments.

Beyond this problem, there was also the problem of the commons. Initially, people were free to venture forth into the world and to use whatever resources were available for the taking. As just discussed, the process of developing the commons resulted in private property and, thus, the increasing closure of the commons. Over time, more and more of the commons has been enclosed as private property has spread. However, wherever commons remain, people are free to view them as open arenas and typically do so in ways that tend to create various tensions among people. The problems arising from conflict over the use of the commons are generally referred to as negative externalities. Among the problems that arise from using the commons are various kinds of water and air pollution. In essence, the commons and the resources available on them are viewed by people as free goods. It should be noted from the outset that the problem associated from using the commons in this way arises from the fact that property ownership is either poorly defined or undefined.

Examples of such abuse are easily observed. For instance, a manufacturer may dump his waste products in a river so that it adversely affects other people living downstream. Or, another producer may emit large amounts of pollutants into the air which fouls the air and causes respiratory problems for people living close by. In yet another example, fishermen may exhaust the fish population of a particular body of water since the ownership of the fish is defined by the catch. In each of these cases, the property rights of the various people involved are not defined clearly enough to avoid conflicts of interests. What is needed is a better means of defining the property of all interests along with the enforcement of the resulting property rights. Of course, as I have already pointed out, there is a potential problem that has always been associated with accomplishing this end. Namely, the power of government which ought to protect property can be used to provide special privilege for some by violating the inherent rights of others. In the case of the use of the commons, users of it who have expended time and effort to develop property may have it legally confiscated by special interests who had no particular attachment to the resources employed and encountered no particular ill because it had been used in some particular way.

With this much said, we can analyze the way the issue of the commons has been handled in the U.S. Prior to 1970, the U.S. policy regarding environmental issues proceeded typically on a case-by-case basis. While there were a few pieces of legislation, the problem associated with pollution and the tragedy of the commons was sorted out through tort litigation by the extension of the common law. In addition, many cases were simply left to private entrepreneurs to resolve. One example of this was the case of buffalo. In the nineteenth century, large buffalo herds existed as part of the commons. As a result, hunters claimed ownership of these animals by killing them. In the course of time, the buffalo were hunted to near extinction. There were no particular laws preventing such action. In fact, the government encouraged it. As the numbers of these animals dwindled, however, the wisdom of saving some of these beasts became obvious.

One development that made this endeavor more feasible was the enclosure of large tracts of land with barbed wire fence. Prior to this innovation, one's potential to own and raise buffalo was severely limited. As the song says, "...buffalo roam." Unlike cows, which are fairly docile creatures, the buffalo were much more adventuresome and rambunctious. When a herd went on the move, it might travel a great distance. Before the introduction of fencing, it was just not practical to attempt to farm buffalo. During the era of the open range, therefore, the buffalo were viewed as more of a nuisance than a resource.

Cattle, on the other hand, could be raised on the open range fairly easily, given their nature and the fact that ownership could be discerned by branding the animals. Branding buffalo would not have worked because of the great distances the animals traveled. As a result, even though more cattle were slaughtered than the buffalo killed in hunts during the same period of time, there was never any danger that the cow might become extinct. Since cattle herds represented a capital investment to their owners, they were not going to be slaughtered all at once. If they were, it would have put the owners out of the cattle business.

However, it is useful to note the difference in the situation once fencing was introduced. Buffalo cannot jump fences any better than cows can and once they are fenced in a particular area their ability to roam is defined and fairly well secured. As a result, fencing made it possible to own and raise buffalo in much the same way that people own and raise cattle. Indeed, that is the case today.

Government action, as this example shows, is not always necessary to remedy observable abuses of the commons. In many cases, the problems arising from such abuses serve to motivate entrepreneurial efforts toward better property rights definition and, thus, workable market solutions to the problems. The only function of government in these cases is to simply affirm and protect the subsequent property rights. At any rate, the combination of entrepreneurial human action combined with successful tort litigation provided the means by which environmental problems were solved until 1970.

The EPA's Assault on Private Property

In 1970, there was a marked shift away from this approach to environmental issues. In that year Congress created the Environmental Protection Agency (EPA). By doing so it abandoned the common law legal tradition of handling such issues in favor of a positive law approach. After creating the EPA, the federal government quickly expanded the number of positive environmental laws with a host of new legislation. Among the new laws passed were the Clean Air Act in 1970, the Clean Water Act in 1972, the Federal Insecticide, Fungicide, and Rodenticide Act in 1972, the Endangered Species Act in 1973, the Safe Drinking Water Act in 1974, and the Resource Conservation and Recovery Act in 1976. Under the terms of each of these acts, authority was given to the EPA to establish rules and regulations for the protection of the environment. In many cases, these laws provide EPA bureaucrats with a good deal of latitude in determining what rules and regulations they will impose. Nonetheless, these rules and regulations have the force of law and anyone who violates them can be prosecuted in a federal court of law for committing a felony.

This change in approach to environmental issues is dramatic. Prior to all these laws and the plethora of EPA rules and regulations, it was largely understood that, without any interference from government, people were free to engage in any business or other activity they might wish to as long as no one could prove their actions were fundamentally harmful to others. However, beginning with these new rules, one could be found guilty of committing a criminal offense, whether or not his actions actually harmed others, if it could be shown that his actions violated some EPA rule. This change in approach to the law has led to a sharp rise in environmental legal cases.

Although pollution issues have continued to improve during the rule of positive environmental law, the rapid expansion of criminal and civil litigation is troubling. The number and complexity of EPA rules and regulations has expanded so rapidly that many people are unaware of what the law actually is.[121] As a result, many people are surprised when government officials target them for prosecution.

The case of John Pozsgai, a truck mechanic, is an

---

[121] For an excellent article on this problem, see Timothy Lynch, "Polluting Our Principles: Prosecutions and the Bill of Rights," *Cato Policy Analysis No. 223*, April 20, 1995.

example.[122] Mr. Pozsgai, found guilty of violating the Clean Water Act in a federal court, was sentenced to three years in prison and fined $202,000. It is hard to imagine the twisting of the law that was used to obtain such a conviction. It seems that Mr. Pozsgai had purchased a piece of land in an industrial section of Morrisville, PA, near Trenton, New Jersey. He bought the property for the purpose of expanding his truck repair business. At the time he purchased the property, it had been used as a dump site and a wide variety of junk littered the land. After purchasing the property, Pozsgai set about to develop it for his purpose and first removed the junk. After that, he began placing fill dirt on the property to correct a flooding problem that occurred whenever it rained heavily in the area. It was this action that brought the wrath of federal bureaucrats who successfully accused Pozsgai of destroying U.S. wetlands. From my point of view, Mr. Pozsgai's actions did not harm anyone else. He should have been left free to develop his own property any way he saw fit. Nevertheless, the federal government successfully made an example of him.

Truthfully, Pozsgai was essentially set up by federal bureaucrats. The rules and regulations that led to his criminal conviction were put in place during George Bush's administration. Shortly after his inauguration in 1989, the EPA and the Army Corps of Engineers released guidelines for wetlands management. "Under the 1989 definition, land that was dry 350 days a year could be classified as a wetland. Even land that had no water on the surface could be classified as a 'federal jurisdictional wetland.' [As] Robert J. Pierce, an Army Corps of Engineers official who helped to write the 1989 manual, later observed, 'Ecologically speaking, the term "wetland" has no meaning: natural systems exist on a hydrologic gradient from ocean to desert. Somewhere in the middle are what society calls wetlands. For regulatory purposes, a wetland is

---

[122] Mr. Pozsgai's story can be found in an article by Paul D. Kamenar, "Private Property Rights: An Endangered Species," *The Freeman*, May 1990.

whatever we decide it is. The type of natural systems that have been defined as wetlands has changed virtually every year for the last decade.'"[123] This sort of arbitrary power placed in the hands of federal authorities is unconscionable. Nevertheless, the government has successfully prosecuted numerous individuals for the crime of using their own property for their own purposes.

In another case, Ronald Rollins, an Idaho farmer, also discovered the bizarre execution of environmental laws the hard way.[124] In 1989, Mr. Rollins was charged with, and found guilty of, violating the Migratory Bird Treaty Act. He evidently did so by applying a registered pesticide to an alfalfa crop he was growing on his property. Subsequently, a flock of geese landed in his field, began eating his alfalfa and died from ingesting the pesticide. Even though Mr. Rollins had applied the pesticide according to instructions and had all the necessary permits for doing so, he was nevertheless found guilty of violating the MBTA because migratory birds were killed in the incident. What is a farmer supposed to do?

In a final example of the EPA's endeavor to defy common sense, during the late 1990s it launched a legal attack on a number of electric utility companies in the Southeast and the Midwest. The lawsuits accused the utilities of violating the Clean Air Act. At issue was the fact that these companies routinely improved their existing plants. As one would expect, in each capital project the companies employed the best technologies available at the time of the investments. As a result, they were able to expand their output at these plants and cut the amounts of pollution at the same time. Indeed, in each case, the utilities had improved the efficiency and cleanliness of their operations. One would have thought that such actions would be praised as they resulted in relatively cheaper electric power with less air pollution.

---

[123] James Bovard, *Lost Rights: The Destruction of American Liberty*, (New York: St. Martin's Press, 1994), pg. 34.
[124] Mr. Rollins story can be found in Timothy Lynch's article, op. cit., pg 13.

158 • Unmasking the Sacred Lies

That, however, is not the way bureaucrats at the EPA saw the matter. Even though the utilities involved in the suit had filed all the necessary forms with the EPA, agency officials sought to impose new regulations retroactively. In essence, the EPA sought to impose new source review guidelines on any investments made by the utilities, whether they were at existing plants or resulting from the construction of new plants. In fact, the rules for new source review are so stringent that they have prevented all sorts of new energy-related plant construction. For instance, as a result of these controls, there has not been a new oil refinery built in the U.S. since the 1970s. This case points to an underlying effort on the part of EPA bureaucrats to increase their power and control over the energy industry.

There are many more examples of the kinds of activities for which the EPA is becoming famous. These, however, sufficiently point out a serious problem with EPA regulation. No enforcement agency can prosecute all violators and must choose which cases to pursue by some value criteria. By selecting these cases to prosecute, it shows that officials at the EPA are at least as concerned about undermining property rights by consolidating political power as they are about addressing the problems of actual pollution. In fact, some of their actions would tend to make the problems of pollution much worse. For instance, as was already noted in the chapter on transportation, the EPA's commitment to smart growth public transit projects will tend to insure greater traffic congestion on the nation's highways. Such congestion will necessarily increase the amount of air pollution because it is a known fact that automobiles pollute more when stuck in stop-and-go traffic than they do when moving at highway speeds. Moreover, since people prefer their automobiles to public transportation, it is clear the DOT's and EPA's efforts to divert gasoline tax dollars to public transit projects will in fact lead to greater congestion.

The Anti-human Philosophy of Environmentalism

Given these facts, one might wonder why EPA officials have moved in this direction. To adequately address this issue, we must look at the origins of the environmental movement. That movement got underway in earnest in America in the 1960s as part of the hippie subculture. This is not to say that there were no environmentalists beforehand, but that a substantial environmental movement did not arise until then. Perhaps many reasons for this exist. Certainly, it gained ground in the hippie subculture which took a stand against the "establishment." In practice this meant agitating against the dominant culture of that day. As such, it took a stand against all things industrial.

While the hippie subculture largely died out (in the end dropping out of society will not put food on one's table), the environmental movement associated with it did not. Once again, there are many reasons for this, but the main one was the presence of water and air pollution. To be sure, the wastes generated in our industrial society produced such pollution, and the presence of it provided an opportunity to address the problems associated with it. Indeed, the wealthier people become, the more concerned they tend to be about the environments in which they live. When people are generally well fed, well clothed, and well housed, they turn their attention to the achievement of other desires and goals. Among these is the desire to live in a more aesthetically pleasing environment. The great economic success of the American economy had brought us to this situation. The tension of the commons had led to the presence of the water and air pollution of that time and this brought the issue to the fore. Moreover, even though progress towards a cleaner environment had been made, the continuing problem of pollution was a real problem that many people could see.

Regrettably, the issue of pollution was co-opted by the hippie subculture movement and set in a direction that insured that the environmental movement would proceed from a point of view that regarded human progress as undesirable. At the heart of the subculture movement of the 1960s was the romanticism of Rousseau who viewed civilization itself as the problem. In his view, man's highest aspirations could be achieved by only by living as savages. Of course this irrational position ignores altogether the rather obvious facts of life that such savage lifestyles are short and brutish and that people living in them are given to extreme poverty and to a bare subsistence lifestyle. In this kind of environment, the person is exposed to all manner of problems arising from poor sanitation, periodic famines, and extremely harsh conditions following various natural disasters. Essentially, such an existence strips the person of any human dignity. In truth, the environmental movement embraces the idea of a golden age in which human beings supposedly lived in harmony with nature. The reality is that this golden age never did exist and never could exist, for it is rooted in a false understanding of the nature mankind and of nature itself.

Despite this fact, the environmental movement continues to be informed and motivated by this kind of irrationalism. Chief among its foundational assumptions is the notion that nature has an intrinsic value. That is, it is assumed that nature is valuable in and of itself apart from uses conceived of and implemented by human action. In essence, the environmentalist is claiming that the earth values itself and that human beings should not be free to co-opt it for their own uses. Put simply, environmentalists see human activity as being inevitably at odds with the rights of the earth and other things in it and, thus, destructive. This has led to the notion that the appropriate course of human action is not to touch, taste, or develop any part of it. In other words, environmentalists aim to put the world off limits, so to speak, in order to maintain what they refer to as a "pristine environment."

Toward that end, they have launched a movement aimed at promoting what they refer to as "sustainable development." Indeed, this phrase has become popularized in recent times in regard to environmental policy discussions. The term is readily thrown around on college campuses today in order to advance a discussion among academics and their students as to what should be done to control the evils of economic growth. The underlying presumption of such a discussion is that too much progress must inevitably result in great pollution and future hardship and, thus, must be controlled. However, such a discussion is very imprecise and must beg the question of what must ultimately be done to sustain life. When the phrase "sustainable development" is examined in this light it becomes obvious very quickly that it represents a human death wish.

At the root of any discussion of "sustainable development" is the idea that economic resources are finite. Aided by the dire warnings of physical scientists, such as Paul Erlich, the environmentalists argue that our way of life cannot be sustained if we use up our so-called non-renewable resources.[125] On the surface this assertion seems correct since we know the earth's size. As a result, there is only a certain amount of stuff on it and in it. For this reason, environmentalists argue that we must conserve this stuff lest we use it all up. However, if this were the problem we face, could we use anything at all? To put the matter another way, if resources are finite such that we might actually exhaust their supply, then should we use them at all? The environmentalist answer is that any use of such resources is non-sustainable. A casual perusal of environmentalist web sites will validate this observation. For example, in an interview appearing on Earth First's web site, Derrick Jensen, an environmentalist writer and speaker responded as follows to a question about the positive aspects of civilization.

> You know, I love Beethoven. I love baseball, except for the designated hitter and the New York Yankees. However, as much as I like the Seattle Mariners and Beethoven, they are not worth killing the planet. At the very least, I think we can be honest about the fact that our way of life from the very beginning has been

---

[125] Erlich's book, *The Population Bomb*, was an important book in promoting environmentalist ideas in the early 1970s.

unsustainable. I asked a friend of mine years ago, "If you could live at any level of technology that you wanted, what would it be?" He said, "That's a really stupid question, Derrick. We can fantasize about whatever we want but the only level of technology that is sustainable is the Stone Age."[126]

Such statements as this by Jensen are routinely made by environmentalists who tend to view human beings as the most problematic inhabitants of planet earth. One of the most telling of the various expressions of hatred of the human race came from biologist David Graber in his L.A. Times review of Bill McKibben's book, *The End of Nature*. In that review, Graber asserted:

> Human happiness, and certainly human fecundity, are not as important as a wild and healthy planet. I know social scientists who remind me that people are part of nature, but it isn't true. Somewhere along the line—at about a million years ago, maybe half that—we quit the contract and became a cancer. We have become a plague upon ourselves and upon the Earth...Until such time as Homo Sapiens should decide to rejoin nature, some of us can only hope for the right virus to come along.[127]

Clearly, individuals like Graber have no regard for other human beings. In truth, such statements should be seen for what they are. Namely, they are the ravings of a morally reprehensible mad man. Moreover, it should be rather obvious that Graber's real problem is that he simply cannot come to grips with the fact that our ability to think, will, and act, coupled with our self-awareness and ability to know something of our own existence, invariably separates us from other animals. The heart of his

[126] Tim Ream, "Hate Civilized," *The Earth First Journal*, Litha 2002, pg. 2.
[127] Robert J. Bidinotto, "Environmentalism: Freedom's Foe for the '90s," *The Freeman*, November 1990, pg. 414.

attack is motivated by an effort to reduce human existence to the animal level.

Regrettably, the environmentalists have made much headway in promoting their ideas in public schools and on college campuses. Indeed, many young people today have bought into this kind of reasoning. For instance, in 2000, the Sierra Club ran an article about a group of tree sitters living in a National Park in Oregon.[128] According to the article, a number of young people had decided to invade the National Park and set up house by building their own tree stands in the tops of several old-growth trees in the forest. The sitters had made use of plywood, mountain climbing gear, polyurethane tarps, camping gear, and plastic jugs to set up housekeeping in these trees. This seems odd to any thinking person since it is not clear what the sitters are protesting.

If they are protesting the cutting down of trees, then using plywood would appear to go against their stated values. Nonetheless, the participants in the protest all believed that they were involved in some worthy mission in life and had sacrificed much to be a part of it. In speaking to the various logical inconsistencies about their activities, one young girl stated rather emphatically, "We drive cars out here. There's a lot of plastic. I like hot showers. I like a roof overhead. But if we don't do this, who will?" The real question is why should any sane person engage in such activities?

In reality, such behavior only makes sense if the environmentalist argument about resources is correct. But, if that is true, then these groups should go all the way and begin living like cavemen without the benefit of anything industrial. Of course they will not do this because many would quickly die. Once again we are confronted with a contradiction in terms since this appears to be exactly the outcome promoted by the environmentalists themselves.

In point of fact, it turns out that the key assertion of

[128] Heather Millar, "Generation Green," *Sierra Magazine*, November/December 2000.

finite resources turns out to be false. In an economic sense, there is simply no rational way to argue that there is a finite amount of resources. While all economists understand the concept of scarcity, they also understand the process of capital accumulation and entrepreneurial action that drives market economies.

Global Warming: A Classic Public Choice Case

Among the many environmental issues that might be considered, the one that has gained the most notoriety recently has been global warming. According to alarmists, planet earth is warming and human activities are largely responsible for the temperature increases. It is argued that the burning of fossil fuels such as coal, natural gas, and oil based products is releasing greenhouse gases, namely carbon dioxide, into the atmosphere and these are causing the rise in temperature. Moreover, it is argued, therefore, that radical changes in human behavior must be made to avert a list of dire consequences that will result from the new warmth. Among the terrible consequences forecasted, are increasing the number of stronger hurricanes, malaria spreading to once colder climates, glaciers and arctic ice melting leading to rising sea levels and coastal flooding, increasing numbers of heat waves, droughts, and wildfires, and the extinction of vast numbers of flora and fauna species.

Despite a well-organized and ubiquitous media campaign to sell the public on this problem, there remain numerous scientists who do not support the call for public action. In fact, many question the scientific justification for it. The alarmist's position suffers from a number of inconvenient facts. The first fact has to do with the importance of carbon dioxide in the current warming trend. It is a known fact that this gas accounts for only about 0.038 percent of earth's atmosphere. Even as a greenhouse gas, carbon dioxide is relatively insignificant. Beyond this fact, human activities account for a very small fraction of carbon dioxide emissions each year. The highest estimate is that our activities account for about four percent of the total emissions in any given year. It is hard, therefore, to believe this is the cause of the current warming trend, but that is what we are being asked to believe. Although it might still be the case that the recent rise in carbon dioxide concentrations is the main cause in the warming, it seems far from certain at the outset given the immense complexity of the earth's climate. Prudent scientists should consider other explanations before jumping to this conclusion.

Despite this fundamental problem with the so-called scientific consensus on human-caused global warming, there are a number of other inconvenient facts. According to the alarmists, manmade warming will cause an increase in the number and strength of hurricanes and they were quick to point to a recent barrage of gulf-coast storms as proof of their position. However, all such data must be viewed in a larger context. William Gray, a leading hurricane expert, dismissed any connection between these storms and global warming.[129] Responding to the alarmists, another scientist, George Taylor, a climatologist at Oregon State University, presented data on the number and intensity of hurricanes for the entire twentieth century. The data revealed no particular trend. In fact, Taylor argues, "...there is no reason to expect increases in hurricanes due to greenhouse warming. Climate models, for all their problems, are unanimous in at least one respect: they predict that most of the future warming will be in high altitudes, in the Polar Regions. This will reduce the north-south temperature gradient and make pole-ward transfer heat less vigorous—a task in which tropical storms play a major role. All other things being equal, a warmer world should have fewer, not more, hurricanes."[130]

The global warming hysteria over the spread of malaria is also unfounded. Years ago, malaria was common in many colder climates. It was wiped out of many regions of the world because

---

[129] Dr. Gray's discussion of the matter can be found in an online podcast at www.tcsdaily.com/multimedia.aspx?id=5.

[130] George Taylor, "Hurricanes and Global Warming: Is There a Link?," TCSDaily article, www.tcsdaily.com.

of the use of DDT, a very effective mosquito pesticide. However, in 1962, Rachael Carson published a book titled, *Silent Spring*, accusing the use of DDT for declining bird populations. The sensational environmental uproar stirred by the book led to a ban on the production and use of this agent in many places. As a result, malaria carrying mosquito populations remained in untreated regions and are on the rebound in others causing the spread of malaria. Although science has since refuted Carson's assertion, the ban on DDT remains in effect and millions of people are needlessly infected by the disease yearly. Literally, millions die from an earlier environmental call-to-action before the scientific work was finished. The current spread of malaria is not only unrelated to global warming, but the entire affair is a good reason to remain skeptical of additional environmental calls to public action in general.

As for many of the other fears of catastrophe that alarmists tell us will befall us as result of global warming, Dr. Richard Lindzen, the Alfred P. Sloan Professor of Atmospheric Science at MIT, warns us against being influenced by the hype. In an editorial following the release of Al Gore's movie, *An Inconvenient Truth*, Lindzen addressed the numerous falsehoods and half-truths associated with the film. In it Lindzen stated,

> To believe [Gore's preferred global-warming template] requires that one ignore the truly inconvenient facts. To take the issue of rising sea levels, these include: that the Arctic was as warm or warmer in 1940; that icebergs have been known since time immemorial; that evidence so far suggests that the Greenland ice sheet is actually growing on average. A likely result of all this is increased pressure pushing ice off the coastal perimeter of that country, which is depicted so ominously in Mr. Gore's movie... Alpine glaciers have been retreating since the early 19th century, and were advancing several centuries before that. Since about 1970, many glaciers have stopped retreating and some are now

advancing. And, frankly, we don't know why.[131]

In making these statements Professor Lindzen is doing what any good scientist does. He is refusing to accept a theory that does not coincide with the facts. Why, then, are so many others rushing to judgment? I think the answer lies in economic theory. It is often said that politics makes for strange bedfellows. There is much truth to that old saying. Many years ago, a colleague of mine, Bruce Yandle, published an article on Baptists and bootleggers. In that article, Yandle observed that a strange political coalition often formed in communities where a referendum was proposed to allow for alcoholic beverage sales. The coalition was typically one forged by Baptists and bootleggers. The former group was motivated by desire to prevent such sales on ideological grounds while the latter group was motivated by money.

This is a key insight into understanding much of the political world. In fact, Professor Yandle recently updated his thesis and applied it to the current issue in an article titled, "Bootleggers, Baptists, and Global Warming."[132] There are many people who are driven by the belief that we are destroying planet earth. The main proponents of this belief are earth worshipers. The central tenet upon which this belief is based is the concept of the intrinsic value of the earth. The idea is the earth is valuable of itself. All human action aimed at altering the planet is, therefore, seen as destructive and evil. A casual examination of their web sites provides the proof that they are anti-economic progress, anti-development, and anti-technology. They are the "Baptists" and they have done a pretty good job of making converts in the public school system and at the academy.

The bootleggers in global warming alarmism include EPA regulators and other government officials, politicians, a collection of scientists, and a cadre of self-interested

---

[131] Richard Lindzen, "Don't Believe the Hype: Al Gore is Wrong. There's no 'Consensus' on Global Warming," *The Wall Street Journal*, July 2, 2006.

[132] Bruce Yandle, "Bootleggers, Baptists, and Global Warming," http://www.perc.org/perc.php?id=193.

businessmen. If you are an EPA employee, the last thing you would want to do is to put yourself out of a job. As air and water quality in the U.S. have improved, however, the need for regulators is diminishing. To continue their jobs EPA, officials must look for new things to regulate to justify their existence. The well-organized effort to list carbon dioxide as a pollutant needing to be regulated is ideal. Such a classification would guarantee the EPA's permanent existence since every breath we take releases the gas into the atmosphere.

Politicians are always looking for ways to expand their power and control, attract campaign financing, and get votes for re-election. To accomplish this, political coalitions must be put together. Global warming is an ideal issue since it provides an excellent opportunity and a means to accomplish all three objectives. As already noted, if carbon dioxide is classified as a pollutant, then every breath we take can be regulated by government. The possible impositions upon the public are unlimited. In that political environment, catering to special interest groups would be an easy thing to do.

For self-serving scientists the issue is an excellent means of promoting their careers. The federal government has essentially monopolized research funding of the sciences in this country. Since most research scientists work as professors at universities and are rewarded for attracting research funding, promoting a government agenda may well be the path to success. Scientists are, therefore, tempted to propose projects that aim to tell the story that the officials want them to tell. The failure to do so would increase the likelihood of being rejected. This would increase the probability losing one's job. This kind of monopolization is not likely to lead to the truth. Rather, it will promote the politically expedient.

Finally, various business enterprises stand to gain financially from new environmental regulations. New restrictions will drive the prices of some resources artificially high. Any company correctly positioned will be able to make large profits as a result. For that reason, such political entrepreneurs make large campaign contributions to ensure that policy decisions promote their businesses.

The categories of people listed above are not mutually exclusive. You are likely to find both "Baptists" and "bootleggers" in each. In all my years studying the subject of political economy, no issue has so thoroughly conformed to the general pattern of public choice theory as this one. Since most people are largely ignorant of the topic, they are easily swayed without realizing the fundamental costs they are imposing on themselves and others. Moreover, the bandwagon is easy because you can think of yourself as a conscientious person doing the right thing. The problem, though, is that public action today will carry tremendous costs and will subject millions if not billions of people to greater poverty as energy prices are driven to unaffordable heights.

Chapter 11: The Lawlessness of Too Many Laws

What are the sacred lies? The first, and biggest lie, is the notion that the institution of government is capable of successfully and adequately addressing all human problems. The truth is that such collectivism hampers human progress because it opens the door for many flagrant abuses of people and their property rights. It provides the greater means by which some people will invariably attempt to make their way in this world off the productive efforts of others. Beyond this foundational lie have been all the particular rationalizations for government meddling into the private affairs of individuals. The widespread belief that government can provide superior education, adequate retirement funds, and a whole host of other goods and services bears witness to the lie. Moreover, the common belief that people have that the government can successfully plan and manage the economy is additional evidence of the success of the lie. All of these beliefs represent the sum total of the sacred lies.

The process of embracing the sacred lies came about in two ways. Some people actively promoted and perpetuated them because they materially benefited from them. Such people have little regard for the truth and are willing to run it over in the streets in order to achieve some temporary gains. They are unprincipled and immoral and engage in their behavior without regard for others. Most people, however, come to embrace the lies in a misguided fashion. It is not so much that they have no regard for the truth, but that they cannot see the detrimental effects of such government activity. They are largely ignorant of the political process and are too busy with their own affairs to devote time to understanding the problems associated with collectivist action. Furthermore, as sound reason is abandoned in favor of empirical analysis as the basis for advocating certain policies, they become ever more likely to succumb to sophistic rhetoric and numbers manipulation. As a result, they become less able to understand the nature of the problems that such policies create and are more likely to embrace further political involvement to correct them.

In the previous chapters I have chronicled America's drift toward the destruction of property rights and the adoption of collectivist policies of various sorts. Although on occasions that movement has been slowed or rolled back, the general direction of legislation has been toward laws and policies that undercut the free market. These policies destroy economic prosperity. Despite the damage done, most people do not see it because it has been masked by the economic advancements that have been made as a result of entrepreneurial action. In other words, a great deal of freedom still remains in America. This has allowed entrepreneurs to pursue numerous endeavors beneficial to the economy. The restrictions imposed, however, have prevented many such endeavors from ever occurring. Since people are unaware of the things that never come to be, they are fooled into believing that material progress is inevitable. Our progress, though, rests on our liberties, which are steadily being eroded away by an elite political class.

It seems to me that one of the great ironies of modern America is that the vast expansion in the legal code of the United States has actually occurred because of the spread of lawlessness. To put the matter more bluntly, it is my opinion that the number of legal restrictions enacted by our Congress has grown as a result of the popular disregard for lawful behavior. To understand why this is true, it is necessary to first understand the nature and purpose of the law itself. When this is done, it will be immediately obvious that much of the modern legal code promotes a false impression about what it means to behave in a civil and lawful fashion. Not only this, but it will also be clear that some of the code is at odds with the established order of nature. In this latter instance it is especially important to point out that government mandates that subvert the natural order of things are in themselves lawless acts regardless of the issue of legality.

The United States was a nation founded upon the belief in natural law. This belief provided a broad consensus among the various groups of people who initially made up the nation. At the time, regardless of one's religious convictions, there was a general agreement that a natural order existed which everyone should respect. Then as now, there were religious disagreements. Nonetheless, the consensus at the time understood that the natural order of things established a standard of behavior. This shared understanding of the natural law centered upon certain fundamental rights.

Unlike many leaders today, the country's Founders shared a very specific view of individual rights. In particular, it was understood that each person had the right to his life, the right to choose his own path in this world, and the right to use his resources or his property to pursue his own ends. By reflecting upon the very make-up of human beings, the Founders, regardless of their religious differences, realized that they shared an agreement among themselves over these three individual rights. The agreement was so pervasive that they could not fathom anyone disputing these foundational human rights. They reasoned that human beings must possess the right to life, because life itself is an essential characteristic of being human and should not be taken away arbitrarily. They reasoned that human beings must also have the right to act, because each person is capable of expressing his own will to act. And, finally, they reasoned that the individual must possess the right to property, because as material creatures we need material possessions to survive. Property, therefore, is indispensable for enabling someone to direct the affairs of his life.

These three rights served as the bedrock upon which the founders of America conceived of government. That is, since each human being possesses these rights, it is necessary that each person's rights be maintained with respect to everyone else. Ideally, they understood that self-government would serve this function better than any other option as long as people made their decisions with a general respect for the rights of others. In fact, they believed that the health of any civilization was determined by the degree to which self-government succeeded. This can be understood by noting that as long as people have a proper regard for others, no outside interference is necessary to secure the peace necessary for the blessings of social cooperation. If people respect and promote the well-being of others, they can live and cooperate among themselves on mutually agreeable terms.

Nevertheless, the founders still recognized a role for state government and civil law. If history teaches us anything, it is that there never has been a time or place where the natural rights of all people were perfectly respected by individual choice alone. In fact, the violation of individual rights is so pervasive that anyone making a careful examination of his own performance will have to confess his failure to fully respect the rights of others. For this reason, some official governmental authority has generally been accepted. People recognize the need to secure their individual rights. But what kind of, and how much, institutional government is needed?

To answer the question, we must first recognize that there are numerous institutions serving the "governmental" function. Primary among these is the family. The family is a natural human institution in which children are born and in which they are raised to adulthood. Parents, being responsible for their children's very existence, are also responsible for teaching them how to behave properly in society. Chief among the many tasks of parents is that of teaching children to respect other people and their property. In pursuing this goal, parents have greater or lesser degrees of success, depending on a number of factors. Fortunately, parents are not alone in this endeavor. In addition to families, there are other institutions that also serve to shape human behavior in positive directions. These include churches, schools, and many other voluntary associations.

These associations tend to restrain displays of gross self-interest that would do violence to the rights of others. The more effective these associations are the more civil society will be. Yet, as effective as social interaction is, there are always some people and some groups of people who disregard others for the purpose of promoting their own interests. Here there is some need for state government, though this need for state action is not of primary importance. In fact, its role is secondary to the functioning of civil society and is needed only when all other remedies have failed. As a result, its role is limited and mainly negative. In particular, the main role of the government is to punish people who threaten civil society with their disregard for the rights of others. In its proper role, government is an institution of last resort.

The problem today is that people have accepted a new conception of what government is. The primary purpose of this institution is to punish wrongdoers within society, promote restitution for people who have been violated, and protect the citizenry from threats made by others outside the civilization. But the popular notion today is that it is government's function to secure the blessings of life by solving the problems common to man. To adopt this view, one must believe that the establishment of legal requirements and restrictions is all that is needed to secure prudent human action and social cooperation. Examples of this kind of thinking abound. For instance, if some individuals prove to be prodigals by failing to save for their financial futures, then what is needed is government action to establish and operate a state-run retirement plan. Or, if some people lack the prudential wisdom of using car seats in transporting their children in their automobiles, then what is needed is a law requiring the use of government-approved child restraints. Following this kind of reasoning, the legal code in America has continued to expand at a very rapid rate as government solutions are sought for the problems of life. As a result of this rapid expansion, the nation's legal code has become highly complex. So extensive has it become, that many parts of it are even contradictory. The size and complexity of the law baffles not only the simple-minded, but also the highly educated. Many very learned people are dumbfounded by the legal restrictions the nation has imposed.

This situation is not desirable for a number of reasons. First, when the vast majority of people do not know what is legal and what is not, the likelihood that they may violate the law is greatly enhanced, even if they desire to behave as law abiding citizens. Yet, because of the sheer size and scope of the law, most people will remain more or less ignorant of it because the cost of obtaining the necessary information about all that is required is too high. As this kind of ignorance of the legal code spreads, people will tend to ascribe less and less significance to it. Increasingly, the law will matter less to people as they go about their lives. This is tantamount to a declining respect for law. As the respect for the law wanes, there will also be a corollary decline in the respect for authority. This disrespect will be enhanced when people observe others being punished for breaking laws they themselves find petty or insignificant. The result is a breakdown of the authority structures of society. This will tend to occur even when those structures are the fundamental pillars upon which civilization is built.

Not only will there be a growing disrespect for authority, but there will also be a decline in morality and virtue among the citizens of a society where the legal code proliferates beyond the bounds of reason. As the legal code expands, the state usurps the authority of the citizenry and of the other institutions in the community that formerly served to promote morally responsible human action. As was already discussed above, institutions such as the family, the church, the schools and other voluntary groups play a crucial role in promoting a standard of moral behavior. If allowed to operate on their own terms, these institutions work fairly well in developing community. However, as the legislature begins to impose more and more restrictions, people tend to become more and more isolated from each other and from these institutions. In this case, the natural social institutions that help the members of society to coalesce together are hamstrung in their efforts. As this happens, immoral behavior escalates because the relationships that might have served to restrain people beforehand are broken. Instead, people tend to gravitate into special interest groups whose aim is to change the law in a particular direction in order to promote their own interests. Since these groups necessarily compete against each other in the political arena, a growing hostility among them arises. This is especially troublesome when some political interest groups begin to shape the law in ways that undercut the individual rights of people in competing groups. In this case, the legal code itself becomes an instrument of immorality. That is, there is nothing that prevents the legal code from being used to violate the rights of others and from being used as the tool by which evil people accomplish their ends. When this happens, the code itself can be deemed lawless. The result of all of this activity is less civility among people and greater lawlessness.

As we have already seen, as the legal code expands, the level of ignorance over its content grows. And, as people become more ignorant of the law, the likelihood that they will violate it increases. When this happens, the actual number of violations will also increase. The more numerous the violations, the more costly it will be to try to enforce the code. Eventually, the number of violations becomes so numerous that it is impossible to adequately administer the law. At this point, the application of the law will become political. When a vast number of people are guilty of violating some portion of the legal code, it is obvious that the state cannot apprehend, prosecute, and punish such large numbers of citizens. Therefore, to execute the laws at all, officials must do so in some discriminatory fashion. Since governmental power is a handy weapon, those who possess it will inevitably use it to punish their political enemies. A good example of this took place during Clinton's initial year in office when several of his appointees suffered defeat for their failure to pay the so-called "nanny tax." Perhaps the most shocking part of this news story for many was the sudden realization that they too had violated the law. They too had failed to withhold and match the social security taxes on their baby sitters as required by the detailed rules of our nation's tax code. Even though it was most likely that a very large number of American citizens had violated this rule, the law served as a convenient weapon to stop several appointments. Of course this is just the tip of the iceberg and both political parties are skilled professionals at wielding the legal code against each other.

Nonetheless, the significant point is that a legal code enforced only for politically expedient ends is an example of lawlessness that also leads to the decline of civilization. For all of these reasons, it is wise to limit not only government but also the number of laws which government enacts. The resulting legal code is then readily known and generally enforced.

Index

G

H

I

J

K

L

M

N